D1087002

BOLERO

THE LIFE OF MAURICE RAVEL

PUBLIC LIBRARY
VTIO OAMAM

Maurice Ravel,
from a photograph by Henri Manuel

BOLERO

THE LIFE OF MAURICE RAVEL

BY

MADELEINE GOSS

"De la musique avant toute chose,
De la musique encore et toujours."
—Verlaine

NEW YORK

HENRY HOLT AND COMPANY

To the memory of my son

ALAN

who, in a sense, inspired this work

CONTENTS

CONTENTS

ILLUSTRATIONS

ILLUSTRATIONS

x

BOLERO
THE LIFE OF MAURICE RAVEL

Ravel au
pupitre
"Boléro"

luc albert

Ravel directing *Bol*...

I

BOLERO

THE foyer of the Opéra-Comique in Paris was filled, one November evening in 1928, with an excited crowd of people. Some still remained in the theater, applauding madly and crying, *"Bis—bis—bravo!!"* The audience, moved to a frenzy by the steady beat of drums and gradually mounting crescendo of sound, were completely under the spell of the stirring music to which they had listened—the first orchestral presentation of Ravel's *Bolero*.

At the back of the hall a woman clutched hysterically at the exit door with both hands. *"Au fou . . ."* she cried. *"Au fou!"*

Yet no one who had watched the little man as he stood on the podium, quietly but with relentless rhythm directing the orchestra, could seriously have accused him of being crazy. On the contrary, he appeared the epitome of unhurried co-ordination. A slender figure, he was dressed in faultless evening clothes almost a shade too

1

perfect. His gray hair gleamed silver in the light, and his narrow, ascetic face, with sharp nose and close-set eyes, showed no emotion. The thin lips were tight pressed, as if trying to shut away all outward expression of the pleasure which the enthusiastic reception of his *Bolero* gave him.

In the artists' foyer a growing crowd waited to acclaim Ravel.

"C'était magnifique, Maurice," a friend cried, seizing him by both hands. "The audience was carried off its feet!"

Ravel smiled ironically. "That was my intention," he replied. "A deliberate attempt, if you like, to work up the emotions."

"Ciel—how you succeeded!" his brother exclaimed, and told him of the woman who had cried *"Au fou!"*

Ravel smiled again. "She is the only one who really understood."

To Ravel's own surprise, his *Bolero* took the musical world of two continents by storm. People from all walks of life—the man in the street as well as the educated music-lover—were completely fascinated by the stirring rhythm of its simple theme. Ravel, whose fame had previously been restricted to a limited number of admirers, became almost overnight a musician of international importance.

The critics, who do not always echo popular opinion,

joined with one accord to marvel at *Bolero*. They spoke of its "irresistible power of bewitchment," and called it "an amazing wager of virtuosity," a "*tour de force* of orchestration." Ravel could not understand this success. (When *Bolero* was in rehearsal he was heard to remark: "*Celui-là, on ne l'entendra jamais aux grands concerts du Dimanche.*" On the contrary, it became such a favorite with concert audiences that some called it "*la Marseillaise des Concerts Classiques.*")

In the United States the success of *Bolero* was even greater than abroad. Toscanini first presented it in the fall of 1929, and the audience was so carried away that it stamped and howled with enthusiasm. Countless performances followed, given by every conceivable combination of instruments from symphony orchestras to jazz bands; it was played at radio concerts and at cabaret shows; it became more popular than so-called "popular music." As a final triumph, Hollywood, whose endorsement is the last word in public favor, used it as the basis of a moving-picture. Believing *Bolero* to be an opera, a film company paid Ravel a fabulous sum for the rights; then, finding that it was only a musical composition, ended by using just the title with the music as background.

Yet to Ravel *Bolero* was one of his least important works. Few will deny that he wrote it with his tongue in his cheek. "*C'est une blague,*" he admitted—a wager (*gageure*) with himself to see how successfully he could develop one simple phrase into a major orchestral composition. In characteristically modest fashion he disclaimed all credit for his extraordinary achievement: "Once the idea of using only one theme was discovered," he said, "any Conservatory student could have done as well. . . ."

The theme of *Bolero* is of little importance; it is the superlative orchestration that makes it a masterpiece. One might expect a work built upon a single phrase to be monotonous and uninteresting; but the contrary is true: the varied coloring and combinations of the different instruments which Ravel has used produce an effect of great variety and richness. There is a proverb in France which says that "the sauce makes the fish" (*la sauce fait passer le poisson*). In the case of *Bolero*, the theme is the fish, and the orchestration the sauce. Ravel reduced the fish to nothing, and by means of the sauce produced a supremely palatable dish. It is the workmanship in this composition which is important, rather than the musical outline, and Ravel asserted that in this respect at least it was one of his most successful compositions. Of it he said:[1]

"I am particularly desirous that there should be no misunderstanding about this work. It constitutes an experiment in a very special and limited direction and should not be suspected of aiming at achieving anything other or more than what it actually does. Before its first performance I issued a warning to the effect that what I had written was a piece lasting seventeen minutes and consisting wholly of 'orchestral tissue without music'—of one long, very gradual crescendo. There are no contrasts, and there is practically no invention save the plan and the manner of execution. The themes are altogether impersonal . . . folk tunes of the usual Spanish-Arabian kind, and (whatever may have been said to the contrary) the orchestral writing is simple and straightforward throughout, without the slightest attempt at virtuosity. . . . I have carried out exactly what I intended, and it is for the listeners to take it or leave it."

Bolero begins softly, and with such ingenuous simplicity that it is hard to believe it can develop into the compelling force of the final climax. First the drums herald the rhythm: *

This beat continues through the entire number with monotonous insistence and a very gradual crescendo. The theme is first played by the flutes alone; a thin, faint echo of the chaos to come, it reminds one of a

* Permission granted by Durand and Company, Paris, and Elkan-Vogel Company, Inc., Philadelphia, Pa., copyright owners, for use of passages from *Bolero* here and on the book jacket, and of the passage from *Rapsodie espagnole* on page 116.

BOLERO

Spanish street boy whistling a popular air as he passes by:

Next, the clarinets take up the refrain, then the bassoons, trumpets, saxophones, horns—each group of instruments in turn developing the haunting melody. The strings play a pizzicato accompaniment, re-enforcing the relentless beat of the drums, and gradually the entire

6

orchestra mounts to an overpowering finale of rhythm and sound.

Rhythm was the real fountainhead of Ravel's art. From the stately tread of his *Pavane pour une Infante défunte* to the frankly jazz swing of later compositions, he is constantly dominated by the fascination of the dance. Spanish rhythms had an especial appeal for him, and *Bolero*—though not, strictly speaking, in traditional style—gives a convincing impression of Spain.

This composition was originally written to fill an order for a Spanish dance number, and Ravel finished it in less than a month. Since he often spent years on a single work, this was an extraordinary achievement in itself. He was never content unless his compositions were perfect. This sense of perfection was the ruling passion of his life—he had a special genius for precise and minute chiseling of musical forms. Stravinsky is said to have called him "the Swiss clock-maker of music" because he composed his scores with the same precise care that a craftsman uses in putting together the intricate parts of a watch. Not a note was placed until after long study to determine just where it belonged.

In his personal life Maurice Ravel was likewise precise in every detail. Small, both in stature and in build, his slender figure was always dressed in the latest and most irreproachable style. No effort was too great for him to make in achieving the effect he sought, whether this was a matter of matching tie, socks, and handkerchief to a certain suit, or of working out the intricate details of a composition.

To those who really know and love Ravel's music it may seem unfortunate that much of his popularity rests on one of his least important works. It should be borne in mind, however, that if it had not been for the success of *Bolero* many people would never even have heard Ravel's name. Because of their interest in this composition large audiences both in the United States and abroad have come to an understanding and appreciation of his more serious works.

Bolero was first presented as a ballet by Mme Ida Rubinstein at the Opéra in Paris. In the early summer of 1928 Mme Rubinstein asked Ravel to orchestrate some numbers from Albéniz' *Ibéria* for a Spanish ballet that she wished to produce. When he started the work he discovered, to his considerable annoyance, that another musician, Fernandéz Arbos, had been given exclusive rights to orchestrate Albéniz' compositions and had already prepared several of them for the dancer Argentina. Ravel therefore decided to write an original work for Mme Rubinstein's ballet. "It will be easier," he said, "than to orchestrate someone else's work." The idea of building a composition from a single theme had interested him for some time. Now he decided to take the opening measures of a popular Spanish dance and work these into a ballet number. In a letter to Joaquin Nin he wrote that he was starting a somewhat singular work: [1]

8

"*pas de forme proprement dite, pas de développement, pas, ou presque pas de modulation; un thème genre Padilla, du rythme et de l'orchestre.*" Bolero, the final outcome of this effort, was in truth "without actual form or development and with scarcely any modulation—a theme '*genre Padilla*'—rhythm and orchestra."

The stage of Mme Rubinstein's ballet was set to represent the interior of an Andalusian inn, with a huge table in the center, and a large lamp hanging directly over it. The scene was like one of Goya's paintings, with deep shadows and brilliant contrasts of light and color. A crowd of gypsies sprawled about in chairs and on the floor, half asleep. In the beginning they seemed unconscious of the music, but as the theme became more and more insistent, Mme Rubinstein, with castanets and a brilliant Spanish shawl, climbed to the table and started to dance. First she moved slowly, in languid rhythm, then with more and more abandon. Gradually the onlooking gypsies began to awaken and sway with the music. Finally the whole company joined in the dance and whirled to a furious climax of motion, sound, and color.

Although *Bolero* was enthusiastically applauded as a ballet, it has achieved even greater success in orchestral performances. Conductors are invariably given an ovation when they present *Bolero*. Ravel called it a "*danse lascive*"; undoubtedly it does have a curious power of stimulating the feelings through its primitive rhythm and increasing tumult of sound, and brings an emotional release to many who hear it.

When Toscanini gave his first presentation of *Bolero* in Paris, the seats—some as high as three hundred francs each—were sold out weeks in advance. Ravel, who seldom went to concerts, was not notified or consulted, and it was only with difficulty that a place was obtained for him at the last moment. As usual, he arrived late, and was obliged to wait in the corridors until the first part of the program was completed. This did not add to his good humor, and when Toscanini started *Bolero* in much faster tempo than the score indicated, Ravel shook his head disapprovingly. Finally he became audibly indignant.

"C'est trois fois trop vite!" he muttered.

When Ravel himself conducted *Bolero*, the beat of his baton never wavered. His arm, like that of an automaton, indicated the movement with unhurried precision: *One-two-three—one-two-three.* . . . The real Spanish bolero rhythm is considerably faster than Ravel has specified. But when this was pointed out to him he replied, *"Cela n'a aucune espèce d'importance."* "The effect," he insisted, "must be achieved solely by the cumulative production of sound and the relentless insistence of monotonous rhythm."

"C'est une danse d'un mouvement très moderne et constamment uniforme, tant par la mélodie et l'harmonie que par le rythme, ce dernier marqué sans cesse par le tambour. Le seul

10

*élément de diversité y est apporté par le crescendo orches-
tral."* [3]*

Toscanini, however, who is a master of effects, feels
that a speedier pace improves *Bolero;* by increasing the
tempo he builds up a stupendous climax. At the concert
in Paris the entire audience rose to its feet, cheering
and applauding.

Knowing that Ravel was in the audience, Toscanini
turned to include him in the ovation and beckoned him
to the stage. But Ravel was outraged. He felt that he
had been humiliated by the liberties which Toscanini
had taken with his work, and he refused to rise or
acknowledge the applause.

Later he went back-stage and had it out with Toscanini.
"You did not play *Bolero* as I wrote it," he said. Tradition has it that the great conductor replied: "If I had
played it as you wrote it, it would have had no success." †

165

Every creative work, whether in the field of literature,
art, or music, reveals in some measure the personality
of its author. In this sense *Bolero* may be said to describe Ravel's own character. To make much out of
nothing—to create a masterpiece from the least possible

* "It is a dance whose movement is very modern and constantly
uniform, as much in its melody and harmony as in its rhythm,
this last marked ceaselessly by the drum. The only element of
variety is provided by the orchestral crescendo."

† It is interesting to note that Ravel's recording of *Bolero* takes
four sides, while Koussevitsky's takes only three.

material—this was typical of his life. But *Bolero* is more than a musical *tour de force:* it contains, in the unexpected modulation near its close, an element of tragic intensity. André Suarèz writes: [4]

Bolero is the musical image of the underlying suffering which perhaps afflicted Ravel all his life, and which at the end became so terrible and cruel. . . . The obsession of the rhythm, the hallucinating insistence of the musical theme, and the deafening violence of its accents create a sort of *Danse Macabre. Bolero* is a confession of the nightmare which haunted Ravel, and of the dark anguish which tormented his soul.

Until Maurice Ravel's tragic death in December 1937, his life and personality remained a complete mystery to the outside world. He shunned publicity and cared nothing for public acclaim; during his last years he lived as a recluse at his country home in Montfort-l'Amaury, just outside of Paris.

He was shy and reserved in character, and those who knew him only slightly considered him cold and aloof from human emotions. But his intimate friends (who were few in number) realized that beneath his outward indifference lay a warm heart and a deep capacity for feeling. They knew that he possessed an excess of temperament rather than a lack of it—a sensitivity hidden but profound, which is evident to those who really understand his works. Secrets of the heart, Ravel felt, are not for the public; emotions must be regulated by intelligence, and any exhibition of them is undignified. While

12

his diffidence often expresses itself in irony, the real tenderness of his nature—and its underlying suffering—can be glimpsed in many of his compositions.

To really understand Ravel it is necessary to know his heritage, which is a strange Basque combination of Spanish ardor and French restraint, together with the precise attention to detail which is characteristic of the Swiss.

II

CHILDHOOD ON THE BASQUE COAST

RAVEL'S ANCESTRY AND PARENTAGE—HIS BIRTH, CHILDHOOD, AND EARLY INTERESTS— HIS MUSICAL BEGINNINGS AND FIRST TEACHERS

AT the extreme southwestern point of France, adjoining St-Jean-de-Luz and separated from it only by a bridge, lies the little village of Ciboure. Before it stretches the Atlantic, and at its back rise the picturesque Pyrenees. It would be hard to find a more romantic spot or one more filled with strange legend and history.

For here is the country of the Basques—a proud people, descended (some say) from the mythical Atlanteans whose continent vanished centuries before history was first recorded. These Basques, who settled both north and south of the Pyrenees, consider themselves a race apart; their language has no kinship with any other European tongue, and their temperament and customs are similarly unique. Neither French nor Spanish, they yet share some of the characteristics of both these peoples, combining cold intellectuality with the love of warmth, color, and rhythm of their southern neighbors.

14

But they are jealous of their independence and do not willingly admit allegiance to either France or Spain.

The men are small and stocky, brown and weather-beaten; they wear the traditional beret and broad, colored sash, and their favorite sports are fishing and the national game of pelota. By nature the Basques are reserved, often taciturn, yet poetical and responsive to beauty, and—above all—extremely proud and sensitive; they feel intensely, yet scorn to show emotion.

It was in the Basque village of Ciboure that Marie Eluarte,* the mother of Maurice Ravel, was born and brought up. Her father was a sailor and fisherman, as had been his father and grandfather before him; they were all devoted to the sea, and also to the mountains that rose so close to their village. Simple folk, but aristocrats in sentiment and fine feeling.

Although the country just north of the Pyrenees belongs to France, the people seem closer in temperament to their southern neighbors. The Eluartes had relatives living in Spain, and when Marie grew older she was sent to visit them. While at Aranjuez, in the Castilian desert region of northern Spain, she met Joseph Ravel, a mining engineer from Switzerland, who was assisting in the construction of a new Spanish railroad. A few months later, in 1874, the young Basque girl and the Swiss mining engineer were married.

Joseph Ravel's family came originally from the little village of Collonges-sous-Salève, near Annecy in the

* The name is sometimes spelled Delouart.

Haute-Savoie. Aimé, father of Joseph, moved from there to Versoix, a small town not far from Geneva, and adopted Swiss nationality. The name Ravel was perhaps originally Ravex, Ravet, or even Ravez (all pronounced alike), for at the time of Joseph's baptism his grandfather's name was entered on the parish registers as François Ravex, while a few years later the record of the latter's death calls him François Ravet.

Many people, especially in the United States, seem to be under the impression that Maurice Ravel was of Jewish ancestry. Roland-Manuel, distinguished biographer of the French composer, believes that this may be due to the fact that his name is similar to Rabbele (little rabbi), and also because Ravel was closely associated with a number of Jewish people during his lifetime, and composed songs in Hebrew style. But actually there is no suggestion in any existing record to indicate that there was Jewish blood on either side of Ravel's family.

After Aimé Ravel moved to Versoix he became, some say, a baker; according to others, a manufacturer of porcelain. He married a Swiss girl, Caroline Grosfort, and they had five children—three daughters and two sons, Joseph and Edouard. The younger son, Edouard, became a well-known painter; his portraits of Joseph and the latter's wife Marie Eluarte still hang in Ravel's study at Montfort-l'Amaury.

Joseph Ravel was deeply interested in music. In his younger days he wanted to be a concert pianist; he attended the Conservatory in Geneva for several years, and eventually won a prize there for his playing. But an equal gift for mechanics and a talent for invention finally turned him to a course in engineering. Before he went to Spain, Joseph Ravel had already invented a machine which could be run with gasoline—a forerunner of the modern automobile.*

When Joseph met Marie Eluarte he was already in his forty-second year, and much older than his wife; but this difference only served to strengthen the bond between them, and their devotion to each other was the firm foundation on which Maurice Ravel's early life was established.

Joseph had expected to take his wife back to Paris soon after their marriage. But when Marie found she was pregnant she wanted to remain with her family in Ciboure until after her child was born. "It is cold and gray in Paris," she said. "Let our infant come into the world here, where Nature is kind and the sun is warm." On March 7, 1875, their son was born in an old Italian-style house facing St-Jean-de-Luz, at 12 Quai de la

* An amusing story is told about this machine by Maurice Delage. In January, 1868, Joseph got permission to try out his *voiture à pétrol* on the Route de la Révolte for a distance of one kilometer, escorted by two policemen on foot. The new invention proved so successful that he was able to go the entire distance to St Denis *and return!* To pacify the *gendarmes*, who could not keep up with the dizzy pace of his "gasoline carriage" (six kilometers per hour was the estimated speed), he promised them as many hot grogs as they could drink, and thus escaped a *contravention.*

Extrait du Registre des baptêmes de la paroisse St Vincent de Ciboure Diocèse de Bayonne

L'an mil huit cent soixante quinze et le treize mars a été baptisé par moi soussigné, vicaire de cette paroisse, Joseph Maurice Ravel, né du mariage légitime de Pierre Joseph Ravel et de Marie Delouart

Le parrain Joseph Maurice Ravel représenté par Simon Goyenague, la marraine Gracieuse Billac qui n'a pas pu signer avec moi

Sinarraga pr. 8e vicaire
Pour copie conforme :
Ciboure, le 9 février 1939
N. Recalde
curé de Ciboure

Ravel's baptismal certificate, copied by the curé of Ciboure

Nivelle,* in Ciboure, Basses-Pyrénées. Here, within sound of the ocean's waves and in the shadow of the Pyrenees, Joseph Maurice Ravel first saw the light of day.

When the child was a few months old the Ravels moved to Paris; and this city remained headquarters for Maurice until the end of his life, although Ciboure and St-Jean-de-Luz were really home to him. Whenever they could afford the journey, the family traveled southward in the summer. Until his last days Ravel returned frequently to the scenes of his earliest memories—to the beautiful Basque country, so close to the rhythms and color of Spain.

Maurice grew into a slender, delicate child (always small for his age) with a mass of black curls and Basque eyes like his mother's, deep-set and close together. He had his mother's gentleness too, and would sit quietly for hours while she told him stories of her youth and people. Folklore and fairy-tales were his favorites. He felt a curious kinship with this shadowy in-between world, and something of this remained with him all through his life. In later years he wove these stories into musical poems of exquisite feeling.

As a child, Maurice loved nothing so much as the fête days in Ciboure, when the village people gathered in the central Place to dance the fandango and make music.

* Now rechristened, in honor of Ciboure's illustrious native son, Quai Maurice Ravel.

He would stand with his mother on the edge of the crowd, watching the dancers and listening with absorbed interest to the guitars and mandolins. The contagious swing of the music stirred a deep response within him, and fostered a feeling for rhythm which became the foundation of his art.

As Maurice grew older he developed a mischievous spirit; he became interested in tricks and magic, and saved his pennies to buy books containing marvels with which to amaze his playmates. Ravel never lost this youthful desire to astonish. It was a quality which endeared him to his friends and appeared as a dominant characteristic of his music.

The small apartment in Paris—many stories above the narrow rue des Martyrs—was meagerly furnished, containing only the barest necessities of life, for Joseph's resources were slender and he was always needing money for his inventions. Yet the Ravels never felt actual privation, and what they lacked in luxuries they made up for in family spirit and genuine devotion to each other.

"You will see, Marie," Father Ravel often said, "some fine day I shall invent a machine that will make us all rich." That day never came, but his wife was satisfied with her lot. She did not care for the luxuries and personal adornments that are dear to most women. For to Marie Ravel her home and her friends—most particularly her children—were enough in themselves.

20

(*upper left*) Marie Eluarte Ravel, mother of Maurice. From a painting
by Ravel's uncle

(*upper right*) Joseph Ravel, father of Maurice

(*lower*) The house in Ciboure where Maurice Ravel was born on March
7, 1875

Maurice, aged twelve, with his brother, Edouard (*rig*

Three years after the family moved to Paris another son was born, whom the Ravels named Edouard after his illustrious uncle, the painter in Switzerland. Edouard inherited his father's mechanical ability to a marked degree. He was musical, too, though his elder brother's talent overshadowed his own gifts. But he was never jealous of Maurice; on the contrary he always felt for him the greatest love and admiration, and no matter how domineering Maurice might be, Edouard followed his older brother's directions without question. "He was *autoritaire* but gentle—with a heart of gold," Edouard said in later years. "Maurice liked to have his own way, but he had to be sure that others considered it the best way too—otherwise his pleasure was spoiled. *Sensibilité folle; égoïsme avec cœur. . . .*" Maurice was equally devoted to Edouard, and the two filled the little apartment with shouts of laughter and high spirits. The neighbors sometimes remonstrated.

"*Petits diables!*" Marie would exclaim, half reprovingly, but with complete pride and affection.

"You are not severe enough," a friend once told her.

Marie smiled in reply. "I would rather that my children loved me than that they should merely respect me."

She was more of a comrade than a mother to her sons. They not only loved her—they adored her; and their father, too, for he made wonderful toys for them, and brought home mechanical marvels for them to look at. Maurice wanted to pull these apart to see just how they worked; he had a passion for machinery. "If I had not been a musician, I should have turned to mechanics," he was often heard to remark: true son of a father who, had he not been an engineer, would have become a musician.

There was a piano in the little apartment, and this was Joseph's most cherished possession. Hardly a day passed without music, for the elder Ravel, who had devoted so much time to the piano in his earlier years, found his greatest enjoyment in playing. Little Maurice would leave his games when his father went to the piano and draw close to listen. Joseph sometimes took him on his knee and let him strike a few notes. He was delighted to find that his son seemed to be gifted with musical talent.

When Maurice was seven his father decided that the boy must have lessons with a capable teacher. The elder Ravel had many musical friends in Paris who often came to the little apartment to make music, and among these was one whom he especially admired, Henri Ghys, composer of the famous *Amaryllis* (*Air Louis XIII*). The latter thought Maurice a little young, but he was willing to try him out. In his diary that evening Ghys wrote:

"*31 Mai, 1882. Je commence aujourd'hui un petit élève Maurice Ravel, qui me paraît intelligent.*" *

* "31 May, 1882. I am today starting a little pupil, Maurice Ravel, who seems to me intelligent."

It was a red-letter day in the Ravel family when Maurice could play and read music well enough to perform duets with his father. Thereafter hardly a day passed without finding father and son together at the piano. When Joseph returned from his work he would hunt up Maurice. "How about a little four-handed Wagner?" The elder Ravel's favorite was the Overture to *Tannhäuser*, and they played it so frequently that Maurice grew heartily tired of the music. (This may have had something to do with his later antipathy to Wagner.)

Although Maurice was gifted, he did not show exceptional promise in those early days, or even for several years to come. This, however, was more fortunate than otherwise, since "child prodigies" so rarely progress beyond their early precocity. His father's unfailing interest and encouragement were perhaps mainly responsible for the ultimate development of Maurice Ravel as an outstanding and unique artist. He himself acknowledges this fact: [1]

"Tout enfant j'étais sensible à la musique. Mon père, beaucoup plus instruit dans cet art que ne le sont la plupart des amateurs, sut développer mes goûts et de bonne heure stimuler mon zèle." *

* "From early childhood I was sensitive to music. My father, much better educated in this art than most amateurs are, knew how to develop my taste and to stimulate my enthusiasm at an early age."

When, presently, Maurice began to attend classes at the Lycée, his first teacher of harmony was Charles-René. This new work fascinated the boy; the development of keys and chords and the intricate mechanics of composition proved as absorbing to him as taking apart and putting together a mechanical toy. Each evening he would hurry through the preparations for his next day's classes at the Lycée in order to work out some particularly complicated task that Maître Charles-René had set him.

This able and wise master required his pupils, in addition to certain prescribed exercises, to write variations on classical themes, and even to compose original pieces of their own. Maurice enjoyed this part of his work best of all, and showed early signs of promise; when he brought his teacher some *Variations on a Chorale by Schumann,* and later a movement of a sonata, Charles-René felt sure that the boy had a future.

"Really interesting efforts," the latter wrote, years later,[2] "which already showed aspirations towards that refined, elevated, and ultra-polished art which today is his noble and constant preoccupation. There has been a real unity in his artistic development; his conception of music is natural to him and not, as in the case of so many others, the result of effort."

In the latter part of the last century, as today, the best possible instruction in France was to be found at the Conservatoire National de Musique. In 1889, when

24

Ravel was fourteen years old, both Henri Ghys and Charles-René felt that he was sufficiently well prepared to fulfil the necessary entrance requirements. Accordingly he was coached for the required audition, and passed the tests successfully.

III

THE PARIS CONSERVATORY
IN RAVEL'S TIME

ITS HISTORY—RAVEL'S TRAINING AND TEACH-
ERS AT THE CONSERVATORY—RICARDO VIÑES
—RAVEL AS A PIANIST—HIS FIRST MEDAL
—EARLY REBELLION AGAINST TRADITION

THE buildings which in Ravel's day housed the Paris Conservatoire National still stand on the rue du Conservatoire. They suggest an old convent, or even a prison, their gates of iron shutting in the stone-paved court through which the students passed to their classrooms. These rooms were dark and cold, and small iron-barred windows added to their prisonlike effect; against the walls were placed hard wooden benches which helped to maintain the rigid discipline and alert attention required of the students. In 1911 these buildings were given up and the institution was moved to 14 rue de Madrid, just behind the Gare St-Lazare, where it still remains.

When the Conservatoire was first founded in 1784, it was housed in what was then known as the Hôtel des Menus-Plaisirs du Roi. Here was established an Ecole

26

Royale de Chant, under the directorship of Gossec; two years later a department of drama was included, and the school became the Ecole Royale de Chant et de Déclamation Lyrique. When the city of Paris decided to establish a municipal band, another section was added, called the Ecole Gratuite de Musique et de la Garde Nationale Parisienne—a lengthy title later shortened to Institut National de Musique. The two sections were eventually combined, and the school acquired its present name: Conservatoire National de Musique et de Déclamation de Paris. This is a free institution maintained by the Government for the training of gifted young musicians.

Sarette, the first director of the institution, was succeeded by a number of famous musicians. First Chérubini, and then Daniel Auber, Ambroise Thomas, Théodore Dubois, and Gabriel Fauré. At the present time Henri Rabaud is head of the institution.

In 1800 Napoleon Bonaparte reorganized the Conservatoire; with various changes and additions it has continued now for over a century and a half, and has been an important factor in the remarkable advance of French music during the past century.

Because of its high reputation, hundreds of students try for the available places each fall. Only those with outstanding talent are chosen, and admission to the Conservatoire has come to be an achievement in itself, while to receive a Premier Prix is the highest honor to which a young musician can aspire.

The Paris Conservatory offers a complete preparation for a musical career; besides instrumental or vocal training, the students are required to have a solid grounding in *solfège*—the "alphabet of music," * and harmony—"music's grammar." Here music is taught like a foreign language, with all its rules and idioms. Yet more important than the actual instruction is the tradition of excellence which influences all those who come within its atmosphere, and sends out the young student thoroughly equipped for the pursuit of his art.

Ravel was to spend fifteen years at the Conservatoire National. He entered the preparatory piano class of Anthiome in 1889 at the age of fourteen, and later graduated into Charles de Bériot's class. In harmony and counterpoint he studied with Emile Pessard, Henri Gédalge, and finally with Gabriel Fauré.

Soon after his entrance into the Paris Conservatory Ravel met a young boy of his own age whose brilliant playing was the envy of all the students in Anthiome's class. That Ricardo Viñes came from Spain was one of the things that attracted Maurice to him. Spain held a special glamour for Marie Ravel's son; she had told him so much about the foster-country of her girlhood that he felt a very real kinship with the Spanish.

Although a Spaniard, Viñes was destined to spend most of his life in Paris, and his friendship with Mau-

---

* Surprisingly enough, Ravel asserted that he had never learned *solfège*, and that he therefore remained all his life a poor sight-reader of music.

rice, begun in the first days of their respective careers, was the longest and most enduring relationship of Ravel's life. Viñes became a celebrated concert pianist, both in Europe and South America (he never visited the United States), and did much, in the early days when Ravel was an unknown young composer, to bring the latter's music before the public.

In those years "modern" music found little favor with audiences still accustomed only to the classics. But Ricardo Viñes ardently championed the young composers and included their works on his programs in spite of opposition. G. Jean-Aubry mentions [1]

the hisses that greeted Viñes when he interpreted, for the first time, Maurice Ravel's *Miroirs*. . . . In ambush behind his moustache, careless of the smiles of the so-called *connaisseurs*, he pursues, calmly and without advertisement, his patient and assured fight to impose that which is worthy. . . . None has accomplished a more ungrateful task, contributed more lively enthusiasm, or given more proofs of an assured taste, in spite of all and of everyone.

Viñes today is a small, bent figure, genial and kindly in disposition, and loved by all his fellow-artists. Gone are the handlebar moustaches, but his eyes are still full of youthful enthusiasm, and in spite of his sixty-four years his playing has much of the brilliance of his earlier days. No one can interpret Ravel's music with quite the same sympathetic understanding as his old comrade of Conservatory classes.

Viñes still retains a vivid picture of the fourteen-year-old Maurice.[2] "He looked like a young Florentine page then," says Viñes; "straight and stiff, with bangs and flowing black hair. *Allure un peu guindée et circonspecte, sérieux, grave, l'esprit orienté vers tout ce qui était poésie, fantaisie, tout ce qui était précieux et rare, paradoxal et raffiné . . . mince figure de Basque au pur profil, gracile, menu, au cou grêle et dégagé, épaules étroites. . . ."* *

Mme Viñes often accompanied her son when he went to visit Maurice, and Marie Ravel was delighted to find someone with whom she could speak the familiar Spanish of her youth, for she felt a little lost in the great city of Paris. The two families became intimately associated— both having musical ambitions for their sons. Ricardo and Maurice spent hours together at the piano, trying every four-hand arrangement they could find—especially those of the modern composers. Nothing pleased the parents more than to listen with fond approval to the music of their gifted sons.

The Ravels lived at that period at 73 rue Pigalle, on a corner overlooking the Place Pigalle. A wide balcony extended around two sides of their sixth-floor apartment, and in warm weather the Ravels, like so many other French families, moved their table outside and ate their meals in the open air. Maurice and Ricardo found endless amusement in looking down at the people in the

* "His gait a little stiff and cautious, his manner serious; inclined by temperament toward the poetic and fanciful, the precious and rare, the paradoxical and refined; his delicate Basque face with its clear profile, his slender neck and narrow shoulders."

street below. The café in the Place Pigalle was a favorite rendezvous for young artists, and models promenaded before the tables, vying with each other for the privilege of posing for the painters. "We would lay wagers, Maurice and I," says Viñes, "as to which artist would choose which model."

At night the stars seemed very close above the balcony, and the two boys, gazing upwards at the constellations, were inspired to study astronomy together. When they wearied of this, Maurice would take his friend into the small salon, lighted with a single, green-shaded oil lamp, and entertain Ricardo with some new trick or sleight-of-hand technique he had just learned, or perhaps build from a box of matches amazing small houses and fragile bridges as intricate as his compositions of later years. He was full of mischief and high spirits.

Most exciting were the evenings when the street fairs were held on the Place Pigalle below. From the vantage point of their corner balcony the two boys could hear the music of the carrousel and watch the crowds milling about in the Place below them. On these evenings the bright lights of the street fair proved more interesting than the stars above. Yet both of these found their place in the pattern of Ravel's life-fabric. The glamour and color of material things often prevails in his music; but the stars are there too, and can be found by those who seek for them.

Maurice felt the greatest admiration and even envy of his companion Ricardo's piano-playing.

"But you could do as well yourself," Viñes often told him, "if only you would work." Maurice, under the stimulus of his friend's urging, would seat himself at the piano—"always very straight and correct, as if glued to the seat"—and begin to practise his scales and exercises. But soon he would lose interest in such dull work and start to improvise original melodies.

Ravel's hands, though narrow, were well adapted to piano-playing: he had long, agile fingers and supple wrists. But he was lazy about his practising. (In later years he left out the lower notes of octaves when he played.) The slightest interruption distracted him. His mother was often in despair over his lack of industry. She even bribed him to work. "Thirty centimes an hour, Maurice—for good, honest practising. . . ."

Each spring when the *Concours* or competition for prizes at the Conservatory approached there was an upheaval in the Ravel family. *"Voici un Concours qui arrive—qu'est-ce-que nous allons faire?"* But at these moments Maurice needed no urging to work. He would practise his contest number with feverish intensity, hoping each time to win one of the coveted prizes.

In 1891, two years after his entry into the Conservatory, the competitions were held—as they still are today—in the concert hall of the Salle du Conservatoire. The auditorium slowly filled with relatives and friends of the young musicians who were to appear, while in the center loge of the first balcony a solemn group of judges awaited the trial.

Each contestant, in the order of the number drawn, was announced in stentorian tones, appeared on the stage, bowed nervously to the judges, and played the contest piece.

"Maurice Ravel, élève de Monsieur Anthiome, deux-ième année. . . ."

Maurice really distinguished himself in the contest piece, playing brilliantly. But he was not so confident about the second part of the contest, when each student was required to read at sight from manuscript. Young Ravel waited anxiously for the final decision of the judges.

"Première medaille—Maurice Ravel. . . ." Yes! he had won a first medal. Maurice was delighted, but principally because of the joy this triumph brought to his beloved father and mother. It was a triumph never repeated—in piano-playing, at least. Ravel could have been a first-class concert pianist if he had wished to work toward such a career. Charles de Bériot, into whose advanced piano class Ravel now graduated, lost all patience with the wayward Maurice. "It is criminal of you to be always last in the class when you *could* be first," he admonished. For the world at large, however, it is fortunate that Ravel lacked ambition to become a piano player. "He did not care for the piano," said Viñes, "but only for Music—*ce qui est très heureux pour nous.*"

His real interest even then was in composition. Emile Pessard, Ravel's first teacher of harmony at the Conservatory, was a liberal who liked to encourage originality

33

in his young pupils—at least within what he considered reasonable limits. Gustave Mouchet, who was in the harmony class at that time, wrote the following description of Pessard's reaction to young Ravel:[3]

Emile Pessard was not too narrowly limited by the rules of harmony; although he taught his disciples the rules and grammar of sounds, he enjoyed stimulating their faculty of composition.

"Bring me your efforts. I shall be interested to see what your musical aspirations are like. You, Ravel—have you nothing to show me?"

Soon afterward Ravel brought a manuscript, entitled, I believe, *Sérénade Blanche*.* Emile Pessard sat down at the piano. We stood around him. After reading the first page the master stopped in surprise.

"You had better play this yourself. You have put in some very strange things here."

Ravel obeyed, and performed admirably this early work of his youth.

"Ah, yes," Pessard commented; "you have produced a very curious effect here. But you seem to be riding fantasies; you must control your thoughts, take fewer liberties. Well—who knows, perhaps you will create a new style for us."

The master, paternal as he was with his students, did not realize how well he prophesied that day.

Young Ravel pleased his teachers with his quick mind and—when he desired—by his expert docility. But at the same time he often startled them with the audacity of his early compositions, and soon he was conspicuous at the Conservatory for the extravagance of his harmonic combinations. Sometimes, while waiting for Maître

* Probably the *Sérénade grotesque*.

Pessard to arrive, Ravel would entertain his classmates by parodying well-known scores or by playing outlandish bits from little-known composers.

He was mischievous by nature, and rebelled against tradition when it refused to permit new interpretations. Massenet was still at this time professor of advanced composition at the Conservatory. Ravel thought the style of this venerable musician too conservative and old-fashioned; his melodies he dismissed as "sugarplums." Later, however, he came to a sincere appreciation of the qualities of the great composer and admired especially Massenet's remarkable orchestrations. He often quoted the latter's celebrated words: *"Pour savoir son métier il faut apprendre le métier des autres."* ("To know one's own trade one must learn the trade of others.")

Ravel's objection to tradition arose not from the fact that he was by nature a rebel (on the contrary he had an unusually precise and order-loving character), but from his belief that the old school placed too much emphasis on cut-and-dried rules—on the "letter" rather than the "spirit" of form. He felt that music should never be constrained to a stiff rigidity, but should always remain supple enough to allow of variation and new developments. He learned, however, through his training at the Conservatory, that a certain number of rules and regulations are necessary—in music as in all things of life. Ravel did not, even in his most revolutionary works, throw tradition and form completely overboard. He used these instead as a ground on which to embroider new patterns with subtle and hitherto unknown color combinations. His art lay in expanding the known rather than in restlessly seeking novelty.

During Maurice Ravel's first year at the Conservatory (1889) the French Government held a "Universal Exposition" in Paris. There Ravel heard the works of Rimsky-Korsakoff, who had been invited to conduct two concerts of his own compositions at the Exposition. The Russians were practically unknown in France at that time, and it was not until some years later that Ravel had an opportunity to hear more of this colorful new music. At the Exposition he also heard a *gamelang* * orchestra from Java, a startling Oriental novelty which intrigued all the musicians of that day with the curious tonal progressions and complicated rhythms of its music. Some critics find a certain resemblance to this Javanese *gambang* in the tinkling bells of Ravel's *Laideronnette, Impératrice des Pagodes*, from the *Ma Mère l'Oye* suite.

In his constant search for new forms, Ravel took to examining the works of the more modern composers of his time; one day in 1890 he found the music of Alexis Emmanuel Chabrier.

* Or *gamelan*, a Javanese orchestra composed of instruments resembling the xylophone and called *gambangs*.

IV

HE BEGINS TO COMPOSE

CHABRIER—SATIE—THEIR INFLUENCE ON RAVEL
—HIS FIRST COMPOSITIONS—"MENUET ANTIQUE"
AND THE "HABANERA"—LITERARY INFLUENCES

RAVEL, discovering Chabrier soon after his entrance into the Conservatoire, was carried away by the originality and brilliance of this musician's works. Here, at last, was what he had been looking for—a new, more vivid, and more effective musical speech. He studied Chabrier's compositions with enthusiasm, and persuaded Ricardo Viñes to learn with him the *Trois valses romantiques* written for four hands.

Both boys were anxious to meet the celebrated composer whose music they admired so much, and when they had mastered the *Trois valses* Maurice suggested: "Let us ask Monsieur Chabrier if he will allow us to play for him, and tell us what he thinks of our interpretation of his waltzes."

Viñes was a little dubious. "Would such a great master waste his time listening to two unknown Conservatory students?" he asked.

But Chabrier was not so unapproachable as they

feared. He received the two sixteen-year-old boys with his usual cordial manner, and listened carefully to their performance of his *Trois valses romantiques*. But he interrupted them so many times, and had such varied and conflicting criticisms to make, that they left the august presence completely bewildered.

Alexis Emmanuel Chabrier was a large man with an exuberant and compelling personality. He overflowed with vitality and good humor, hearty laughter, and a keen and ready wit. If his critics accused him of sentimentality, or even occasionally reproached his "exquisite bad taste," they could not deny the brilliance and novelty of his music.

He spent fifteen years in the Ministry of the Interior before he was able to devote himself exclusively to what had always been his major interest—the composing of music. *"Quinze ans perdus,"* he often said with regret. But when he once started, his development was so rapid that he more than made up for the "fifteen lost years." Chabrier maintained that he was principally self-taught. Certainly he was not bound by convention or tradition, and he brought to his art a wealth of originality and imagination which did much to develop the modern school of French music.

He was an intimate friend of most of the leading writers and painters of his day, among them Verlaine, Monet, Manet, and Renoir—all reactionaries from the old school; and Chabrier's music reflects the color and impressionism of these artists.

His humorous fancy is evident in a number of songs with curious titles: "Ballade des gros dindons," "Pastorale des cochons roses," "Villanelle des petits canards." But he is principally known for his opera *Le Roi malgré lui* (which had been performed but three times when the Opéra-Comique burned down in 1887) and the suite *España*, a masterpiece of rich and colorful orchestration.

Chabrier's influence on Ravel is evident in a number of the latter's earlier works. *Sérénade grotesque*, the first composition of which any record remains (written in 1893), bears a strong impression of the older composer's style. Ravel himself admitted that Chabrier's music had had a definite effect on the *Pavane pour une Infante défunte* and was one of the most important factors of his early development.

All through the years of Maurice's musical training, Joseph Ravel followed his son's development with keenest interest. He shared the boy's enthusiasm for the newer composers. One day, when Maurice returned to his home from the Conservatoire, he found his father in conversation with a stranger. Carelessly dressed, with pointed beard and humorous eyes, the man seemed to fill the salon of the little apartment.

"My son is much interested in modern music," the elder Ravel said as he introduced Maurice.

"They call *me* modern," Erik Satie replied, laughing ironically, "but not in a complimentary way."

Satie was notorious among the musicians of his day.

Talented but extremely eccentric, he seemed to delight in defying all tradition, and he liked to outrage the conservatives by strange dissonances and the weird titles he gave his compositions: *Pieces in the form of a Pear, Gymnopédies, Podophthalma, Holuthuries, Unappetizing Chorale, Grimaces of a Midsummer Night's Dream*—to quote only a few of his strange fancies. ("Affectedly humorous," some call these works.)

Born in Honfleur in 1866, of a Scottish-English mother and French father, Erik Alfred Satie showed early signs of rebellion against the world and its ways. His favorite companion was his uncle "See-Bird," an original character whose unconventional ways scandalized the community.

When he was twelve, young Erik moved to Paris. There his father conducted a modest music-publishing establishment and planned to have his son take up a musical career. In 1879 Erik was entered in the Conservatoire; but he was completely unhappy in this "vast building, very uncomfortable and ugly to look at: a sort of local penitentiary without anything agreeable within —or, for that matter, without." [1] He was too rebellious, while at the Conservatory, to settle down to the hard work necessary for a good musical foundation, and in later years he had cause to regret the indolence of those early years.

To escape military service, young Satie exposed himself to cold and nearly died of bronchitis. During his convalescence he read Flaubert's *Salammbô*, and was

inspired to write his most famous suite: *Gymnopédies.**
Some of his compositions were favorably received, but
his failures were more numerous than his successes, and
as the years went by he was reduced to bitterest poverty.
He moved to Arceuil in the suburbs, where in micro-
scopic lodgings (*comme un placard*) he spent a long
period of complete discouragement and depression. It
was here—so it is said—at a modest café near his lodgings that the elder Ravel first met him.

In time Satie came to the conclusion that his failure
to achieve success was due to his lack of early training. ✓
In 1905, therefore, when he was nearly forty years old,
he decided to begin all over again, and entered the Schola
Cantorum, the most rigid and severe of all the schools
of composition. Many of his friends warned him against
this plan, among them Debussy, who was a close friend
of Satie's until a misunderstanding separated them in
1917. "Take care," Debussy told him. "You are playing
a dangerous game. At your age one doesn't change one's
skin." But Satie replied, *"Si je rate, tant pis! C'est que
je n'avais rien dans le ventre."* † [2]

Satie was one of the most original characters that ever
lived. *"Resté toute sa vie un enfant naïf, qui s'étonne de
tout,"* ‡ he was ironical but kindly, quick to take offense,

---

* Dr. Stokowski has recently made a recording of Satie's first
and second *Gymnopédies* (Victor record No. 1965).

† "If I fail, so much the worse!—It will prove that I have no
guts."

‡ "All his life he remained a naïve child whom everything
astonished."

but equally quick to forgive. He adored animals and children, and often drew upon his meager resources to take the poor children of his neighborhood on excursions into the country.

Maurice Ravel became one of Erik Satie's most ardent admirers. The budding young composer never tired of playing and studying Satie's fascinating compositions. One day he took the *Gymnopédies* to his class at the Conservatoire, to astonish and bewilder his comrades with their strange harmonies. Maître Pessard, arriving unexpectedly, could not believe his ears.

"What are you playing, Monsieur Ravel?" he demanded, seizing the manuscript disapprovingly. *"Gymnopédies?* Humph—what does that mean? Erik Satie!!"* He threw the music into a corner. "You had better leave such trash alone, my boy. It does not belong in the realm of true music."

But not all the criticism from older and more conservative musicians—even that of some of his own companions—could shake Ravel's allegiance to Satie. The latter, though a little ironical, was secretly gratified by this devotion. *"Il me certifie toutes les fois que je le vois qu'il me doit beaucoup. Moi je veux bien."* * [3]

In 1910, when Ravel himself was a noted composer, he gave a concert of Satie's works under the auspices of the Société Musicale Indépendante.† The program contained the following appreciation:

* "Every time I see him he protests that he owes me much."
† For a description of the S. M. I. see Chapter XI.

Erik Satie occupies a really exceptional place in the history of contemporary art. A little in advance of his time, this recluse has written a number of genial pages. These works, unfortunately not numerous, surprise one by their modern vocabulary and by the semiprophetic character of certain harmonic discoveries.

This concert marked the beginning of a certain vogue for Satie's works, particularly among the younger musicians; and the "Groupe des Six"—who in 1910 were the leading "moderns"—acclaimed him as their leader. But the unfortunate Satie did not profit much materially. His poverty remained lamentable. He could not even attend some of the concerts given in his honor because he had no suitable clothes to wear. Hailed "Prince of Musicians" he replied, *"Le Prince des Musiciens ne sera pas riche, le pauvre!"* In spite, however, of his own failure to achieve outstanding success, Erik Satie has probably had more to do with shaping the course of the younger French composers who followed him than has any other man—except, perhaps, Debussy.

It was during the period when Ravel discovered Satie that he wrote his first songs: "Ballade de la reine morte d'aimer" (1894) and "Un grand sommeil noir" (1895). Both of these show Satie's influence, particularly in the choice of their names. (Later works also contain echoes of this influence—notably "Sainte" and the *Entretiens de la Belle et la Bête* in *Ma Mère l'Oye*.)

Ravel's earliest compositions—the *Sérénade grotesque*

and the two songs—have never been published. He himself may have felt them to be only a beginning, unworthy
of presenting to the public. Or he may have wondered
whether, after all, the good Maître Pessard was not right
—whether too much originality might not be a drawback
in the writing of music. At any rate his next work shows
more regard for the conventional style.

Ravel's first published composition, the *Menuet antique,* appeared in 1895, and was dedicated to his friend
Ricardo Viñes. Though in this work Ravel follows the
classical more closely, its title is somewhat of a paradox
—forerunner of the curious contradictions he was so
fond of throughout his life; but there are certain striking
innovations that deny the austere implication of this title,
and the *Menuet* is an excellent example of Ravel's ability
to achieve originality and the unusual *within* the restrictions of form. Roland-Manuel calls it "a conflict between scholastic severity and bold exploration . . . a
quarrel between order and adventure." [4] We can imagine
the twenty-year-old Maurice trying to conform obediently
to the precepts of his teachers, yet unable to resist a few
dissonant chords and "modern" harmonies.

Ravel had, strictly speaking, no *"œuvres de jeunesse."*
All of his compositions, from his earliest printed works
to the amazing concertos for piano and orchestra of his
last years, show a perfection that labels them as masterpieces. When he was little more than a boy, still in
Maître Pessard's class, and with only limited experience
in composition, he wrote one of his most delicate and

perfect works—the *Habanera*—"an example, probably unique, of a great artist who reveals himself entire in the first page he publishes." [5] Ravel had a special affection for this composition; perhaps it reminded him of his childhood days—of lazy hours spent in watching the fishermen on the Basque coast. *Habanera* appeared first in a group with another number, *Entre cloches*. Twelve years later he orchestrated it as a part of his famous *Rapsodie espagnole;* and in addition he arranged it as a vocal number ("Vocalise en forme d'Habanera").

With the success of *Menuet antique* and *Habanera* behind him, young Maurice Ravel decided to give up the idea of a concert career and devote himself entirely to composition. He was filled with insatiable curiosity about everything musical, and sought inspiration for his work in every direction. The composers who had the greatest influence on his early career were Schumann, Liszt, Chopin, and Weber. But these proved to be less important to his development than Chabrier and Satie.

During the impressionable years of his adolescence Ravel became an ardent reader.* He discovered the poets; Mallarmé, Verlaine, and Baudelaire ("*les poètes maudits*") entranced him by their deep sensitivity to music. (He later composed songs to a number of their poems.) Baudelaire, whose famous *Fleurs du Mal* cre-

---

* Ravel was always a great reader, but, owing to his paradoxical nature, he liked to *appear* indifferent to literature. The books in his home were jealously hidden away, and only his most intimate friends knew how much time he spent in reading.

ated such a sensation when they first appeared in 1860, appealed especially to Ravel, and he chose as motto a quotation from one of this poet's works: *"L'inspiration n'est que la récompense du travail quotidien."* *

Edgar Allan Poe was another of Ravel's favorite authors. He thought at one time of setting to music "The Fall of the House of Usher," but this plan never materialized. "The Raven" he called "a musical composition with words instead of notes," and spoke admiringly of the perfection of its balance. "True balance is the union of intellect and feeling," Ravel always insisted. In literature as well as in music he was always more interested in how things were constructed than in the finished product. He preferred depth to breadth, and small details to large horizons. Poe's *Philosophy of Composition* † and *Poetic Principle* attracted him because of their analytic character.

In these early years everything was grist to young Maurice Ravel's mill. Books that he read, music that he heard and studied, and life itself were the materials he utilized for the perfecting of his art. Throughout this period he was struggling to find himself. Not only his arduous training at the Conservatory, but also his study of the "revolutionary moderns" (of all, indeed, that was strange and unusual in the realm of music) and his own experimenting in new fields—all these advanced his

* "Inspiration is but the recompense of daily labor."

† Another title by which this work is known is *How I Wrote the Raven.*

46

development and brought him—in 1897—to Henri Gédalge's course in fugue and counterpoint at the Conservatory. At the same time he entered the class in advanced composition of the great master of his time, Gabriel Fauré.*

* Not to be confused with J.-B. Faure, composer of "The Palms."

V

GABRIEL FAURÉ AND HIS INFLUENCE ON RAVEL

FAURÉ AS MAN AND TEACHER——THE SOCIÉTÉ NATIONALE
DE MUSIQUE——"SITES AURICULAIRES"——ITS FAILURE——
"OVERTURE TO SHÉHÉRAZADE" AND CRITICISMS——
EARLY SONGS——"PAVANE POUR UNE INFANTE DÉFUNTE"

RAVEL spent several years in the class of Henri
Gédalge. His natural interest in mechanics and in the
intricate development of harmonic forms made him an
intelligent and conscientious worker in this difficult
course, for he realized that it is not possible to be a
master of composition without a thorough grounding in
counterpoint. In later years he said that he owed much
of his most valuable training to Henri Gédalge. But of
all Ravel's teachers Gabriel Fauré was to have the greatest influence.

It is unfortunate that Fauré's music is so little known
outside of his own country,* for many of his compatri-
ots believe him to be one of the greatest, if not the great-

* An increasing number of gramophone records are being made
of Fauré's works, and this will doubtless cause his music to become
better known in England and the United States.

est, of French composers. His music is essentially French: elegant and restrained, full of grace and clarity, and never pretentious or overwhelming.

Gabriel Fauré, the youngest son of a family of six children, was born in 1845. His ancestors do not seem to have been musically inclined; his grandfather and great-grandfather were butchers, and his father a schoolteacher. When Gabriel was four years of age, the Faurés moved to Montgauzy and were lodged in a wing of the school where his father taught. In later years Fauré recalled the beautiful garden and the chapel that adjoined the school building. He loved the music of the church, and when he was eight years old his father took him to Paris and placed him in the Ecole Niedermeyer, a school of religious music.

Young Fauré was docile and industrious, though he was a far better student in music than in his other studies. He had a gentle and philosophical nature—solitary and given to day-dreaming. The Ecole Niedermeyer proved an excellent antidote to this tendency. The pupils were obliged to practise all at once in one large room—fifteen students and fifteen pianos: a drastic training in practical concentration.

In 1860 Saint-Saëns, then a young man of twenty-five, came to teach at the Ecole Niedermeyer. He proved a great inspiration to the youthful Fauré, and became the latter's lifelong friend. *"Mon gros chat,"* Saint-Saëns called him affectionately.

When he was twenty, Fauré obtained a post as organist at Rennes, and during the years that followed he returned to Paris and was successively organist at St-Honoré-d'Eylau, St-Sulpice, and finally at the Madeleine. During this period he composed a number of songs and chamber-music works, and also was appointed music critic on the *Figaro*. He liked to amuse himself and his friends by writing parodies of sonnets. . . .[1]

Je regardais passer l'omnibus sur le pont
*Avec cet air pensif que les omnibus ont.**

In 1877 Fauré traveled with Saint-Saëns to Weimar and there met Franz Liszt. A few years later he made the acquaintance of Wagner; but the latter's music overwhelmed him with its volume of sound and its tendency to grandiloquence. He had, by nature, a horror of overemphasis, which he thought denoted lack of taste, and preferred the clear and quiet measures of his own music. *Poète de l'intimité* he has been called. His maxim was: *Faire peu de bruit, mais dire beaucoup de choses.*†

Fauré's *Requiem*, perhaps his greatest composition, was written just after his father's death, in 1866. *Penelope*, a "lyrical drama," came twenty years later. But he is principally known for his piano and chamber-music works. All of Fauré's compositions are filled with delicate beauty and poetic charm; they also contain harmonic innovations which were original and even daring

---

* I watched the omnibus cross the bridge
With that pensive air that omnibuses have.
† "Make little noise, but say a lot."

for their time, though these are never startling enough to jar the sensibilities of classic-minded listeners.

In 1896, Fauré was appointed professor of advanced composition at the Conservatoire National, and in 1905 became director of that institution. At this time the great tragedy of his life began: he discovered that—like Beethoven and Smetana—he was losing his hearing. At first he tried to conceal his increasing deafness, and only his wife knew of the torment he endured. He wrote to her from Switzerland: [2]

I am overwhelmed by this affliction that has struck me in what it is most important I should preserve intact . . . I am constantly weighed down by a frightful cloak of misery and discouragement.

A curiously diabolical distortion added to Fauré's distress: the lower tones of music came to him a third higher, while the upper notes sounded a third lower. He endured his affliction without complaint, but eventually it became so evident that in 1919 he was asked to resign from the Conservatoire. Though he was then made a Chevalier of the Legion of Honor, this hardly compensated him for what seemed a humiliating reflection on his integrity as an artist. He lived five years longer, and in spite of his misfortune continued to compose. The last work of his life, the String Quartet written when he was eighty and finished only a few weeks before his death, is one of his finest compositions.

Gabriel Fauré was the most gentle and unpretentious

of men. As his deafness increased, his music—like Beethoven's—reached new horizons and sounded greater
depths. All through his life he was true to his ideal: *Ne
jamais écrire pour le plaisir, par facilité ou par habileté.
N'écrire que ce qui s'impose, ce que l'on entend en soi.** [3]

When Fauré first came to the Conservatoire in 1896,
to succeed the illustrious Massenet who had held the
chair of advanced composition for close to twenty years,
he brought a new and more liberal atmosphere to the
musty schoolrooms of that institution. His class, instead
of being the traditional instruction-room, was more like
a charming salon where as host he received the most brilliant of the younger musicians, and listened with kindly
interest to their compositions. He suggested rather than
criticized, while the rare quality of his artistic understanding was an inspiration to all those fortunate enough
to come under his influence. Although he himself was a
product of the old school, Fauré had an open mind and
a keen interest in modern forms, and he liked to encourage creativeness in his pupils.

He could, at times, be severe in his censure; but he
was always ready to change his opinion if he found that
his first impression had been too hasty. Once he criticized
relentlessly a composition that Ravel brought him. At
the next lesson, however, fearing that he might have

---

* Never to write for pleasure, facility, or cleverness. To write
only what is insistent, what is heard within oneself.

Ricardo Viñes

Gabriel Fauré,
from a painting by John Singer Sargent, 1889

been too harsh in his judgment, he asked to see the manuscript again.

"But I should blame myself," Ravel told him, "if I even mentioned this work to you again—you found it so detestable."

"I may have been mistaken," replied the liberal-minded master.[4]

Fauré recognized Ravel's unusual ability, and gave him many suggestions (*conseils d'artiste*) which were of invaluable help to the young composer's development. It was undoubtedly Fauré's influence that was responsible for the brilliant *Jeux d'eau* and the String Quartet. Ravel acknowledged this debt in his dedication of both compositions to *"mon cher maître G. Fauré."* When, in 1922, two years before Fauré's death, the *Revue Musicale* published a special number in honor of the great musician, Ravel's contribution was a *Berceuse sur le nom de Gabriel Fauré.*

A year after he entered Fauré's class—in March 1898—Ravel's music received its first public presentation at a concert of the Société Nationale de Musique. This society had been founded in 1871 by Saint-Saëns, Massenet, Fauré, and others, "to aid the production and the popularization of all serious works, whether published or unpublished, of French composers; to encourage and bring to light all musical endeavor, whatever form it may take, provided there is evidence of high artistic aspiration on the author's part." Concerts were given every other Saturday night in various Paris halls—

most frequently in the old Salle Pleyel in the rue Roche-chouart (later demolished and rebuilt in the rue du Fau-bourg St-Honoré). All the leading French composers of the period took part, and through the medium of these concerts were able to make their music known to the public.

Ricardo Viñes, now in his early twenties, was well launched on a successful concert career. As has been said, he was Ravel's most intimate friend and had the greatest admiration for the young composer's music. When, therefore, he was asked to play at a Société Na-tionale concert (earlier than the concert mentioned in Chapter IV), he included one of Maurice's works on his program.

Ravel had recently combined the exquisite *Habanera* with another number, *Entre cloches,* in a suite whose name *Sites auriculaires* * recalled Satie's fanciful titles. He had written this for two pianos, four hands, and Marthe Dron was chosen to play the second part with Viñes at the other piano.

The first public hearing of a young artist's work is a moment of great emotion for him. He sits in the audience watching and wondering. . . . "How will it be per-formed? Will they like it? Will it be over their heads— too modern?" Maurice waited anxiously to see how the audience would receive his compositions.

But alas! *Sites auriculaires* proved a dismal failure.

* Literally, "Landscapes of Sound."

Viñes and Mlle Dron were playing on a new instrument recently invented by Pleyel: the "two pianos in one," built in the form of a square, the convex curve of one piano fitting into the concave curve of the other. Though the two artists thus faced each other, their manuscripts stood on the racks in such a position that neither player could see the other. Now *Entre cloches* contains several syncopated passages of "cross rhythms" alternating between the two pianos; and Viñes and Mlle Dron, unable to give each other the necessary signals, suddenly discovered that they were playing these alternating chords *together*. As a result, the music—daring enough when played right—became a succession of terrible discords. The audience was indignant at this "massacre of sound" and expressed disapproval in no uncertain terms, while the critics unanimously condemned Ravel's work. Even the *Habanera,* so popular in its later forms, received hardly a word of commendation.

Maurice did not reproach his friend with this sad if unavoidable blunder, and Viñes hardly suspected what a keen disappointment the failure meant to the young composer. Ravel was always reserved and aloof, and never allowed his feelings to be seen. Now, like a true artist, he forgot his defeat by plunging into new work—the *Overture to Shéhérazade.*

He had recently read a French version of *The Arabian Nights* by Galland, and was inspired by its colorful and dramatic fantasy to set it to music. He had originally intended to write a complete opera; at this time, however, he got no further than the overture.

Although his first hearing had been so unsuccessful, the Société Nationale gave Ravel another opportunity to be heard a year later, and invited him to conduct his *Overture to Shéhérazade* for one of their concerts. Now, he hoped, he would be able to redeem the unfortunate impression made by his *Sites auriculaires*. The leading critics were to be present—among them the distinguished Pierre Lalo—and altogether this was the most important event of the young composer's career thus far.

But again the performance was a failure. The audience were not only unable to appreciate *Shéhérazade;* worse, they were openly amused. Cat-calls came from the gallery, whistling and booing. . . .

The critics tore his music to pieces unmercifully, and Pierre Lalo was especially indignant: [5]

Monsieur Maurice Ravel is a young pupil from the Conservatory, over whom his comrades and his professors make a great fuss. If this is what M. Ravel believes to be an Overture "constructed on the classical form," we must agree that M. Ravel has a great deal of imagination. His style reminds one in its structure of Grieg, more still of Rimsky-Korsakoff or Balakireff. There is the same incoherence in the general plan and in the relation of the tones; but the characteristics already striking enough in the models are carried to an excess by the pupil.

Even at this early date, however, Ravel felt sure of his own powers. He told his friend Henri Février—a fellow student at the Conservatoire—that he knew what he wanted to do and was sure he could accomplish it. (*"J'ai trouvé ce que je veux dire, et je le réaliserai."*) Since the critics were not far-sighted enough to understand what he was trying to say, he decided to disregard them and work only to satisfy his own inner urge. He was by nature detached and rather ironical in manner; the public failure of his early works intensified his diffidence, which became his armor against criticism and eventually developed into a very real contempt for outside opinion.

The *Sites auriculaires* and the *Overture to Shéhérazade* were never published, though fragments of both are to be found in later compositions. Ravel himself did not think much of the *Overture*. He declared that it was *"mal fichue et pleine de gammes par tons entiers. Il y en avait même tant que j'en fus dégouté pour la vie."* * [6] But the *Shéhérazade* idea still intrigued him, and in 1903 he again used the title and certain themes in a suite of three songs.

Ravel had composed several songs since his early "Ballade de la reine morte d'aimer" and "Un grand sommeil noir." "Sainte," written in 1896 when he was only twenty-one, he dedicated "to Mme E. Bonniot, née Mallarmé." In this song a slow progression of chords interprets the dim religious atmosphere of Mallarmé's poem, while the voice, in a dreamy reverie, sings of an

---

* "A sorry thing full of whole-tone scales, of which there are so many that I'm off them for life."

ancient cathedral with stained-glass windows, where the silent Saint stands in a niche of gilded wood:

Musicienne du silence. . . .

Ravel ends the composition on an unresolved ninth chord, which leaves a curious impression of irony, or questioning.

Two charming songs called "Deux épigrammes" (words by Marot) followed, in 1898. "D'Anne qui me jecta de la neige" recalls the stately pageantry of a court of the Renaissance period, while "D'Anne jouant de l'espinette" is in lighter style. These were sung at a Société Nationale concert in 1900 by Monsieur Hardy Thé. "Si morne," written at this same time on a poem by Verhaeren, has remained unpublished.

The first of Ravel's compositions to be really favorably received was the *Pavane pour une Infante défunte.* This delicate portrayal of an old Spanish court dance, with stately measures that conceal a depth of tender and restrained emotion, has made a vivid appeal to the popular imagination.

The pavane is an ancient court dance which originated in about the sixteenth century either in Italy or in Spain. Some say that the name comes from the Latin *pavo* (French *paon*) meaning peacock. The pavane was performed at the weddings of young girls of high estate, and on feast days to entertain the King and Queen. It was a slow dance, lasting just long enough to permit the dancers to circle the hall three times.

PAVANE POUR UNE INFANTE DÉFUNTE

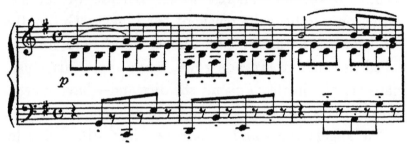

Ravel said that the title of his *Pavane* had no especial meaning; he merely "liked the sound of the words." But many stories have been woven about this composition. In a *Conte bleu* Raymond Schwab wrote a vivid picture of the "*Infante Porquéporqué*, after the *Pavane pour une Infante défunte*, by Maurice Ravel, to whom this tale is dedicated."

In this story, Mademoiselle Parceque (the Infante Porquéporqué) in a gown of blue brocade dances before the King on her tenth birthday the *Pavane* which has been especially composed for her and which she has been practising since she was able to walk. The performance is a triumph, but the little Infante pays no heed, and retires silently to her apartment. From that day she ceases to take any interest in the outside world, but wishes only to hear the music of her *Pavane*. Gradually she becomes paralysed and almost blind, and finally, robed in her blue brocade gown, while the Court musicians are playing her *Pavane*, she dies and—having been of exemplary piety—goes straight to heaven.

The angels guide and sustain her, but, still trying to hear the music of her *Pavane*, she bends toward the earth. They take her to St. Cecilia; the little Infante, however, is unable to enjoy the good Saint's celestial melodies. Blind and paralysed, only hearing remains to her; but the mightiest tones of heaven leave her insensible. All she wishes is to hear her own *Pavane*. . . .

The slow tempo of the *Pavane pour une Infante défunte* is sometimes exaggerated by those who wish to emphasize its mournful character. Ravel once listened to a child who plodded through the composition with industrious but uninspired effort.

"*Ecoutez, mon enfant,*" he said gently. "*Rappelez-vous une autre fois que j'ai écrit une* Pavane pour une Infante défunte—*mais pas une* Pavane défunte pour une Infante!" * [7]

Ravel himself did not have a very high opinion of this composition. He considered it meager in outline and too

* "Listen, my child—what I wrote is a *Pavane for a Dead Princess*, not a *Dead Pavane for a Princess!*" .

much affected by Chabrier's influence. In later years he said that he "could see only its faults and none of its virtues." And Roland-Manuel remarks that it "will win for Ravel the admiration of young ladies who do not play the piano very well."

Written in the closing year of the nineteenth century, the *Pavane* also marks the end of the first period in Ravel's life. To this belong the unpublished works: *Sérénade grotesque*, "Ballade de la reine morte d'aimer," "Un grand sommeil noir," *Sites auriculaires*, the *Overture to Shéhérazade*, the songs "Sainte," "Deux Epigrammes," and "Si morne," the *Menuet antique*, and the *Pavane pour une Infante défunte*. In all these works, melodious and perfect though they seem, he was still trying to find himself and to develop his own essential idiom.

Now, at the beginning of the new century, with a thorough training as foundation, sympathetic guidance, and the stimulation of new friends to inspire him, Ravel was ready to begin the second part of his career, a period that brought to full development his special and unique contribution to the world of music.

VI

FAILURE — AND SUCCESS

HISTORY OF THE PRIX DE ROME—RAVEL'S FIRST COMPE-
TITION, AND WINNING OF SECOND PRIZE—LATER COM-
PETITIONS AND FINAL REFUSAL—"JEUX D'EAU"—STRING
QUARTET—THE THREE "SHÉHÉRAZADE" SONGS

RAVEL had been nearly four years in Gabriel Fauré's
class when he decided to enter the competition for the
most important prize given at the Conservatoire National:
the Grand Prix de Rome.

In 1666 an "Académie de France" had been established in Rome under the auspices of the French Government for the training of painters, sculptors, and archi-
tects. When Napoleon came into power he added a musical department to this academy, the jurisdiction of which
was placed under the Conservatoire National.

Each year a competition for the Prix de Rome is held
at the Paris Conservatory, and the winner is awarded a
four-year scholarship, with residence at the famous Villa
Medici on the Pincian Hill in Rome. During this time he
lives at the expense of the French Government, and must
devote himself to composition, submitting a certain number of works called *Envois de Rome*.

Candidates for the *Grand Prix de Rome de Composi-*

tion Musicale must first go through a preliminary or eliminative test. Those who are selected are placed *en loge*—in isolated retreat—there to set to music the poem (or, as it is called, Cantata) which has been officially selected by the jury. At the end of the period (usually about four weeks) the works of the contestants are publicly performed, and the prizes awarded.

Many of France's most distinguished composers have received the Prix de Rome. Among these are Berlioz (1830), Gounod (1839), Massenet (1863), Debussy (1884), Bizet (1857), Charpentier (1887), Rabaud (1894), Florent Schmitt (1900), Paul Paray (1911), Marcel Dupré (1914), and Jacques Ibert (1919). It is interesting, however, that for the last twenty years the prize has not gone to any composer who has since become eminent.

In the spring of 1901 the usual announcement appeared on the Bulletin Board of the Conservatoire:

Le Concours d'Essai pour le Grand Prix de Rome de Composition Musicale aura lieu au Palais de Compiègne: entrée en Loge le—mai, sortie le—juin. Jugement au Conservatoire.

Le Concours définitif aura également lieu au Palais de Compiègne: entrée en Loge le—mai, sortie le—juin. Jugement préparatoire au Conservatoire. Jugement définitif à l'institut le—juillet.

Each year the judges select a new cantata which the contestants must set to music during their month's retreat. In 1901 their choice fell on a poem by Fernand Beissier called *Myrrha*.

FAILURE—AND SUCCESS

Trained under Fauré and Emile Pessard (himself winner of the Prix de Rome in 1866), Ravel had high hopes of gaining first prize. The financial reward would have meant much both to him and to his family, but even more important would have been the four years of security at the beautiful Villa Medici in Rome, surrounded by the most talented young men of the day. Here he would have had an opportunity to work in an atmosphere of quiet inspiration far different from the restricted quarters of the Paris apartment on the boulevard Pereire, where the Ravels then lived.

He passed the preliminary examinations in May of 1901 and entered *en loge* with four other contestants. An interesting old photograph shows the young composer at the Palace of Compiègne during an intermission of this retreat. He stands at the head of the steps, aloof and distinguished, his carefully trimmed *favoris* and elegant waistcoat in marked contrast to the careless appearance of the other contestants.

Ravel set himself with enthusiasm to the composition of *Myrrha*. Music flowed from his pen like water. In a letter to his friend Lucien Garbau he wrote: [1] *"Il m'a été révélé une chose bien curieuse: c'est que je possède un robinet mélodique . . . et qu'il en coule de la musique sans aucun effort."* *

Ravel finished his preliminary writing among the first,

* "A very curious thing has been revealed to me: that I possess a musical hydrant . . . and that music flows from it without any effort."

64

ı intermission during the contest for the Prix de Rome in 1901. Ra
stands at the head of the steps.

Ravel with his famous beard. About 1905.
Photograph by Pierre Petit

but he put off the orchestration until the time limit of the retreat was almost up. To Ravel, time was never a matter of importance. He excelled in disregarding it, and throughout his life this characteristic was a never-ending source of exasperation to his friends.

In this instance his procrastination was perhaps responsible, at least in part, for his failure to win the *Premier Grand Prix*. He admitted his delinquency: [2] *"Bien que ma composition fût terminée l'une des premières, j'étais arrivé à me mettre en retard et il ne m'était resté que fort peu de temps pour mon orchestre, qui s'en est trouvé quelque peu bâclé."* *

Aside from the rather sketchy orchestration, however, Ravel's contribution had another and, in the jury's opinion, more serious defect. The poem *Myrrha* was a sentimentally written affair, and Ravel could not resist burlesquing some of its passages, treating them as slow waltzes in operetta style. This found favor with some of the judges (Massenet among them), who suggested that Ravel's composition should be awarded first prize. But the majority were indignant at what they considered a lack of respect for the importance of the event and the seriousness of the subject, and the jury finally accorded first place to the work of André Caplet. Ravel was given second prize, but this minor glory—merely a gold medal

* "Although my composition was finished among the first, I managed to delay until there was very little time left for my orchestration—which, as a result, was more or less thrown together."

—carried no financial reward. *"C'est à recommencer,"* he said; *"voilà tout!"*

Ravel tried for the Prix de Rome again in 1902 and 1903. But neither his cantata *Alcyone* nor, the following year, *Alyssa* received a recompense. His friends were indignant, and even Fauré did not hesitate to voice his resentment. For by this time Ravel was beginning to be known as one of the most promising of the younger composers.

Two years later, when Ravel was close to the age limit of thirty, he made a last effort to win the Prix de Rome. This time he was not even passed in the preliminary tests. The judges, to whom the classical tradition was more important than originality, had evidently decided that this young upstart was too dangerous a radical to be admitted into the inner circle which the competition of Rome represented. Their arbitrary decision aroused a storm of protest in the musical circles of Paris. Everyone took sides in the dispute over the *affaire Ravel.* Pamphlets were printed, and even the newspapers rose in Ravel's defense. The judges were openly accused of partiality, and such a scandal followed that Dubois, director of the Conservatory, finally resigned, and Fauré took his place. The famous French author Romain Rolland sent to M. Paul Léon this letter of protest: [3]

I read in the papers that there is no *"question Ravel."* I believe it my duty to tell you . . . that this question does exist, and cannot be evaded. In this affair I am entirely disinterested. I am not a friend of Ravel. I may even say that I am not personally sympathetic with his subtle and overrefined art. But what justice compels me to say is that Ravel is not only a student of promise—he is already one of the most outstanding of the younger Masters of our school, which does not have many such. I do not doubt for an instant the good faith of the judges; I do not challenge it. But this is rather a condemnation for all time of these juries; and I cannot understand why one should persist in keeping a school in Rome if it is to close its doors to those rare artists who have originality—to a man like Ravel, who has established himself at the concerts of the Société Nationale through works far more important than those required for an examination. Such a musician did honor to the competition; and even if by some unhappy chance (which I should find it difficult to explain) his compositions seemed inferior to those of the other contestants, he should nevertheless be received outside the *concours*. It is a case rather analogous to that of Berlioz. Ravel comes to the *examen de Rome* not as a pupil, but as a composer who has already proved himself. I admire the composers who dared to judge him. Who shall judge them in their turn?

Forgive me for mixing up in an affair that does not concern me. It is everyone's duty to protest against a decision which, even though technically just, wounds real justice and art. . . .

The contention over the *affaire Ravel* really marked the beginning of Maurice's popularity, especially among the younger musicians, who felt that the issue involved was fundamentally a conflict between the limited, tradition-bound ideas of the old school and the freer, unprejudiced viewpoint of the modern.

Only Ravel himself remained apparently unmoved through the controversy. But inwardly he was deeply affected, and when years later the French Government offered him the Legion of Honor, he would not accept it. Three times this honor was proposed to him; but Ravel had not forgotten that this same Government, as head of the Conservatoire National, had in a sense been responsible for his early humiliation, and he refused to consider the decoration.

In 1901, at the time when Ravel first competed for the Prix de Rome, he composed one of his most popular numbers. First a pianist, second a composer—at least in his earlier years—he was especially interested in writing for his chosen instrument. *Jeux d'eau* appeared on the horizon like a miniature but dazzling display of fireworks. A verse by H. de Régnier, beginning *"Dieu fluvial riant de l'eau qui le chatouille,"* captured Ravel's imagination—so quickly fired by the fantastic—and he developed the theme into a marvel of descriptive craftsmanship that proved the foundation for a new technique of the piano. *Jeux d'eau* scintillates with the splash of rainbow fountains and rippling waterfalls, where "the fluvial god laughs at the water that tickles him." Ravel said of this composition: [4]

"Cette pièce, inspirée du bruit de l'eau et des sons musicaux que font entendre les jets d'eau, les cascades et les ruisseaux, est fondée sur deux motifs à la façon d'un premier temps de sonate, sans toutefois s'assujettir au plan tonal classique." *

* "This piece, inspired by the sound of water and the music of fountains, cascades, and streams, is founded on two motifs, after the fashion of the first movement of a sonata, without, however, being subjected to the classical plan."

Ravel, only twenty-six at this time, hardly realized the value of his own work. He could not imagine that *Jeux d'eau* might achieve international importance. He told his publisher, Demets, that copyrights would not be necessary, and as a result there are in the United States alone a number of different editions of this composition.

In 1902, on April 5th, Ricardo Viñes played *Jeux d'eau* and *Pavane pour une Infante défunte* at a concert of the Société Nationale. This time the audience was pleased—if not enthusiastic. At last the tide had turned in favor of the young musician. . . .

This tide of popular approval swelled to considerable proportions when, in 1904, Ravel's String Quartet was given its first presentation by the Heyman Quartet. Now at last, the critics were favorably disposed; they hailed the Quartet as a masterpiece. Roland-Manuel, in his first study of Ravel, says: [5]

On March 5th, 1904, at the Schola Cantorum, the Société Nationale revealed to an enthusiastic public the Quartet in F— a miracle of grace and tenderness, a marvelous jewel of polyphony which knew how to submit to the requirements of the classical form without manifesting any of its restrictions. "The composition of a string quartet," M. Vincent d'Indy has excellently remarked, "demands such mastery that many musicians excel in this form only at the end of their career." Maurice Ravel's Quartet in F, work of a twenty-eight-year-old musician, placed its author, in 1905, in the foremost rank of French musicians. . . . Ingenious and at the same time subtle . . . the Quartet is the ardent, the splendid effort of youth confident of its force.

The Quartet has four movements, all of them filled with melodies of great lyrical beauty. In the first three movements these are woven together with delicacy and tenderness, while the last part contains passages of great vigor and passion.

The *Quatuor à cordes* was dedicated to Fauré, but Ravel's "dear master" did not at first appreciate its qualities. He criticized it severely, especially the last movement, which he considered too disconnected and short. Debussy, on the other hand, congratulated the young musician and wrote: "*Au nom des dieux de la musique et du mien, ne touchez à rien de ce que vous avez écrit de votre quatuor.*" *

Although the *Overture to Shéhérazade* had not been a success, Ravel's interest in the *Arabian Nights* story was revived by his encounter with some new poetry by Tristan Klingsor. This talented young Frenchman, whose real name was Tristan Leclère, having fallen victim to the oriental seduction of the Russians, had just issued a series of poems under the title *Schéhérazade* †—poems which, though in blank verse, were filled with rhythm. It is probably this rhythmic quality that appealed to Ravel and made him wish to set three of the poems to music. At his request, Klingsor read *Schéhérazade* aloud to him several times so that he might get the feeling of

* "In the name of the gods of music and of my own, do not touch one thing in your Quartet."
† The title of the poems is so spelled; the title that Ravel used for his songs is spelled "Shéhérazade."

the words. Curiously enough, however, the verses that he chose for setting—"L'Asie," "La Flûte enchantée," and "L'Indifférent"—are the least musical of the group, descriptive in their content rather than lyrical.

These three songs, each complete in itself and differing from the others in form, have been compared to a three-panel Persian miniature rich in color and detail. In them can be seen the amazing variety of Ravel's orchestration: he used the instruments as a painter uses the colors on his palette, and was constantly experimenting with new combinations and subtle tone effects.

Undoubtedly, Ravel's orchestration was influenced by the Russians, but there is little in his "Shéhérazade" to suggest Rimsky-Korsakoff's famous suite of the same name. Where Korsakoff is brilliant, almost too dazzling, sometimes even barbaric, Ravel remains the epitome of refinement. His "Shéhérazade" reveals passion and a certain sensuousness, but these are always restrained and controlled by a fastidious temperament.

As with all of Ravel's songs, these settings of the Klingsor poems show his effort to adapt spoken language to music in a natural and unforced way, and prove that he was here, as always, more interested in interpreting the meaning of the words than in bending the text to an arbitrary musical setting. The major part of the action is given to the accompaniment, while the voice follows and interprets the words. This treatment is especially marked in "L'Asie" (*"vieux pays merveilleux des contes*

71

de nourrice"). Here the soprano sings of her desire to visit the Orient in a ship "which unfolds its purple sails like an immense night bird in a golden sky." The orchestra, its strings scintillating and its wood winds melodious, creates an atmosphere of fairy-tale enchantment as the singer tells, one by one, of all the wonders of Asia that she wishes she might see. (*"Je voudrais voir la Perse, et l'Inde et puis la Chine."* *) Harp glissandos introduce a description of China, with its "large-bellied mandarins under their parasols, and princesses with delicate hands."

> *Je voudrais voir des pauvres et des reines;*
> *Je voudrais voir des roses et du sang;*
> *Je voudrais voir mourir d'amour ou bien de haine.*†

"La Flûte enchantée" is the story of a young slave whose master sleeps. She sings:

> *L'ombre est douce et mon maître dort,*
> *Coiffé d'un bonnet conique de soie*
> *Et son long nez jaune en sa barbe blanche.*
> *Mais moi, je suis éveillée encor.*‡

Through the gentle murmur of muted strings comes the

---

* I should like to see Persia, India, and China.
† I should like to see poor souls and queens;
  I should like to see roses and blood;
  I should like to see death from love or from hate.
‡ The shade is cool, and my master sleeps,
  Capped with a conical bonnet of silk
  And his long yellow nose in his white beard.
  But I am still awake.

flute serenade of her lover, mysterious and seductive in its appeal:

> *Il me semble que chaque note s'envole*
> *De la flûte vers ma joue*
> *Comme un mystérieux baiser.**

The final song of the trilogy—"L'Indifférent"—tells of a graceful young stranger who passes by the door singing in a charming though unknown tongue—*"comme une musique fausse."* But he will not enter . . . he passes on. The song ends in a mood of plaintive melancholy.

* It seems to me that every note flutters
From the flute to my cheek
Like a mysterious kiss. . . .

VII

LES APACHES

PARIS AT THE TURN OF THE CENTURY—THE
SOCIÉTÉ DES APACHES—RAVEL'S FRIENDS AND
ASSOCIATES—INFLUENCE OF THE RUSSIANS—
"MIROIRS"—"LE NOËL DES JOUETS"—"SONATINE"

PARIS, during the end of the nineteenth and beginning
of the twentieth centuries, moved at a far different tempo
from the present day. It was not only a question of loco-
motion—of leisurely fiacres in contrast to speeding taxis
—but rather a matter of temperament and interests. The
young people of that time were less occupied with sports,
racing, and cocktail parties, and more concerned with
fine arts, politics, and intellectual discussions. Art in par-
ticular was their passion—even, it might be said, their
religion—whether in the field of painting, sculpture,
writing, or music. And they were all searching for new
forms, throwing overboard—often ruthlessly—the traditions and ideals of earlier periods.

These years marked a great flowering of the arts in
France, and the development of new lines in almost
every field. Cézanne, Monet, Gauguin, Van Gogh had
broken away from the more formal styles of painting.

74

Rodin's powerful sermons in stone opened a new era in sculpture. Verlaine and Mallarmé were discovering different idioms in poetry, and Satie and Debussy a new language of music.

Innovation was the cry of the day—originality at any price. "We are tired of the old forms," they insisted; "let us be 'different'—no matter what the sacrifice." Those who still clung to the old classics were contemptuously dismissed as *bourgeois*—"middle-class"—not necessarily in social position, but in artistic taste. The young intelligentsia took a malicious pleasure in startling these conservatives (*"épater le bourgeois . . ."*). It was a pose, if you wish, but back of it was the blind, pushing force of new growth seeking to break through the cocoon of outworn tradition.

Montmartre and the Quartier Latin were headquarters of these ardent young priests of the new religion. They were all poor—riches, they felt, were deadening to artistic perception; and creative work, regardless of worldly acclaim, was their creed. A group of these young writers, painters, and musicians met frequently at the apartment of a painter named Paul Sordes, who lived in the rue Dulong, high above Montmartre. Ravel made his acquaintance early in the new century, and through him met the artists who were Sordes' companions.

Maurice now found an atmosphere completely congenial to his tastes. He had always been diffident in his friendships, but the appreciative understanding of these young intellectuals broke down his reserves and supplied a stimulus which inspired him to the most productive period of his career. Eventually this group banded together in a society, and the name they adopted was chosen as the result of a casual incident.

Late one evening, as Ravel and Viñes were crossing a narrow street in Montmartre on their way to Sordes' studio, a rough-looking man bumped into the pair. *"Attention les Apaches!"* he growled, rudely pushing them to one side.

"Apache" was a term of insult popular at that time in Paris, applied to a group in the underworld—social outcasts who had no respect for law or order. Instead of resenting the incident, however, Ravel and Viñes were rather amused. "That's a good name for you, Maurice," Viñes commented as they went on; "at least, the critics would say so," he added, for his companion was already known as a "musical outlaw."

"If I am an outlaw," retorted Ravel, "then so are you —so are all of us, for that matter. . . ."

When they told their friends of this encounter, the others seized upon the name Apache. " 'Société des Apaches'!" they exclaimed. "That's what we will call ourselves." They were, in truth, all more or less outlaws, these young men who gathered at Paul Sordes' studio— at least in the sense that their artistic ideas were not those accepted by conventional society. The name *Apache* appealed to them as a symbol of emancipation.

Paul Sordes was a genial, fair-haired young man who, in addition to his talent for painting, was a musician of considerable ability. He had a passion for Ravel's music, and tried to capture in the colors of his paintings the subtle musical effects of his friend Maurice. The Apaches called Sordes *le Ravel de la palette,* but because of his indolence he never achieved special renown in either painting or music.

Ricardo Viñes—long-faced, with handlebar moustache and fingers always itching for piano keys—was a favorite with the group. Amiable and enthusiastic, he charmed them with his playing or talked interminably in Spanish-flavored French. Léon-Paul Fargue, writer and critic, was one of the original Apaches. Fargue's tardiness was proverbial (*retardataire perpetuel!*). He usually arrived at midnight—or later; if invited for dinner, he appeared (possibly) in time for dessert, announcing that he had already dined, and then proceeded to consume a full meal in reverse order—*"plûtot que d'avouer qu-il est dix heures et qu'il est simplement en retard. . . ."* * [1]

Maurice Delage, eager devotee of music (later to become a pupil of Ravel's and his closest, most devoted friend), joined the group in 1903. Tristan Klingsor, the painter and poet already mentioned, was another distinguished member, and Calvocoressi, an energetic charac-

---

* "Rather than admit that it is ten o'clock and that he is simply late."

ter half-French half-Greek. Calvocoressi spoke many languages and was noted for his translations of operas into French—the list included *Boris Godunov*. (Ravel some years later set to music five folk-songs that Calvocoressi had transcribed from the Greek.) Charles Sordes, white-haired brother of Paul; Pierre Haour, poet; Chadeigne, chorus director at the Opéra; the painter Edouard Benedictus; Inghelbrecht, and Séguy, and a number of others all belonged to this group and united with the rest in common revolt against the "old-timers" who had nothing but criticism for the younger generation. Other outstanding members included Florent Schmitt, Roger-Ducasse, André Caplet, Manuel de Falla, the Abbé Petit, and Igor Stravinsky. And in 1911, Roland-Manuel, one of Ravel's pupils and later his most important biographer, joined the Apaches.

In marked contrast to the exuberant natures of most of his brother Apaches, Ravel's quiet reserve stood out with dignified distinction. He seldom entered into his friends' discussions, usually preferring to listen and keep his reflections to himself. He was at this time between twenty-five and thirty years of age, a slender young man of less than medium height, whose personal appearance seemed to be his chief concern. His shirts were the marvel of his companions, and the elegance of his barbering was repeated in the faultless precision of his attire. Those who knew him only in later years would never have suspected that the bearded young man who

Ricardo Viñes and Ravel

LE BELVÉDÈRE

MONTFORT L'AMAURY (S.&O.)

15/3/22

Facsimile of a letter from Ravel to Viñes

frequented Paul Sordes' apartment was the Ravel of *Bolero* fame. For to the sweeping *favoris* of Conservatory renown had succeeded a luxuriant beard, carefully trimmed according to the whim of the moment. He was, as Roland-Manuel says: [2]

the complete type of dandy *Baudelairien:* elegant indifference, horror of triviality and all effusions of sentiment. . . . [He had] the proud reserve of all those who carry a message whose secret has not yet been revealed.

Ravel, for all his natural diffidence, was full of fun and laughter, and loved nothing so much as to amuse and astonish his comrades. The famous black beard furnished him with all manner of disguises. One week he would trim it in a point—Van Dyke style; at another time he parted it in the middle and cut it square like the beard of the Emperor Francis Joseph. There seemed no end to the ingenious transformations he managed to achieve.

Among the painters most particularly favored by the Apaches was Dégas, celebrated for his portraits of ballet dancers, or *"tu-tus"* as they were called in the slang of the day. Ravel convulsed his friends, on more than one occasion, by dressing in ballet costume, with bodice stuffed to give him a well-rounded figure (*"faux-seins"*) and the famous beard adding a strangely exotic touch. He could amuse his friends with burlesqued pirouettes (*faire les pointes*), though as a ballroom dancer he was stiff and self-conscious. Nothing delighted him more, however, than to watch others dance, whether in a ballet on the stage or to a jazz band in a night club. Rhythm—in music or in dancing—held a never-ending fascination for Maurice Ravel.

Russian music was little known in Paris at this time, and the "Old Guard" considered it barbaric and unworthy of serious notice. The Apaches, however—always seeking for originality and new expressions—seized upon this music with its strong oriental flavor and played all the scores they could get their hands on. Rimsky-Korsakoff, César Cui, Balakireff, Moussorgsky, and Borodin—the "Russian Five"—became their most absorbing interest.

One evening towards midnight Sordes brought out the score of Borodin's Second Symphony arranged for four hands, and he and Delage attacked it with a vigor which nearly brought down the roof—as well as the neighbors —on top of their heads. "It was," said Klingsor, "*un magnifique tumulte.* . . ." The powerful opening to this symphony impressed them all so greatly that they decided to adopt it as a rally call.

While the Apaches were not, in the real sense of the word, a secret society, they had certain signs and passwords personal to themselves. ("Gomez de Riquet" was the name they gave to a wholly imaginary person who provided them with an excuse for escaping from bores.) The first eight notes from Borodin's Second Symphony became a private means of identification. Whenever an

Apache wanted to attract the attention of a fellow member he would whistle the chosen theme:

In crowded streets, at the theater, or following a concert when an enthusiastic group lingered so long that the weary concierge turned out the lights, the familiar rally call brought the Apaches together. *"La Symphonie de Borodine remplace le gaz,"* said Calvocoressi.

In 1904 the Société des Apaches moved to Auteuil, where Maurice Delage had rented a studio at the back of a quiet old garden on the rue de Civry, not too far distant from the *Ceinture* railway. This studio, originally a small pavilion built for the Paris Exposition of 1900 and later moved to Auteuil, consisted of one large room, and was meagerly furnished with a piano and a few chairs. Delage's bed, attached perpendicularly to the inner door of a closet, could be let down into the room after the last Apache had departed—at two A.M. or later. . . . A small *salamandre* provided the only heat. (Léon-Paul Fargue, who was always chilly—*frileux*—insisted that Delage used a candle for fuel.)

Later a second piano was added—more important to the Apaches than heat or elaborate furnishings. Now they were able to make music to their hearts' content, without fear of disturbing the neighbors. All-night sessions were frequent, for often Ravel and his friends missed the last train back to Paris on the Ceinture, and it was more agreeable to play the piano than to sleep on the floor.

Delage's *pavilion* became headquarters for most of the young intelligentsia of the day. Here they gathered—away from all feminine interference—to make music, hold long discussions on the artistic and political questions of the day, and most important of all to read or play their own writings and compositions. They were full of enthusiasm, gay spirits, and *joie de vivre. "Nous étions heureux, cultivés, et insolents,"* says Fargue.

One evening Ravel arrived at the studio with a thin, creased roll of music; he unrolled and smoothed this out with more than usual care, as if he realized that it was something quite precious, and played for his companions a new piano number just composed: *Oiseaux tristes*—the first of a charming suite called *Miroirs,* though in the printed version it is listed second. Each of the five pieces in the suite is dedicated to one of the Apaches: *Noctuelles* to Léon-Paul Fargue; *Oiseaux tristes* to Viñes; *Une Barque sur l'océan* to Paul Sordes; *Alborada del Gracioso* to Calvocoressi, and *La Vallée des cloches* to Maurice Delage.

Miroirs shows the influence of Ravel's new and stimulating environment; it contains richer harmonizations and a broader development than his earlier works. The title is a revelation of one of Ravel's guiding principles: to him the greatest art was a *reflection* of reality rather than an exact duplication of the original. He believed that Man's interpretation of Nature has more value than the thing *per se*. For this reason he took a certain pride in being what he called "artificial"—that is, in transforming material into a more exalted state by means of his own labor. He was more interested in his emotions themselves, expressed through his music, than in the scenes that inspired those emotions. *Miroirs* is reality seen in a mirror—that mirror which is the musician's soul.

Ravel considered *Oiseaux tristes* the "most typical" of the group. It represented, he said, birds lost in a dark forest during the hottest hours of summer. Léon Vallas describes *Noctuelles* as "an inextricable mass of curves drowned in a sonorous flood of audacious intervals which interrupt the fluttering of nocturnal butterflies." The *Alborada del Gracioso* is the most popular of the suite. Its brilliant and effective virtuosity has a special appeal for pianists, and Ravel's later orchestration has made it a favorite with concert audiences. The critics called *Une Barque sur l'océan* "disconcerting"— [3]

like a succession of colors imposed on a drawing hardly sketched. Colors, however, full of richness, vivacity, and extraordinary precision. . . . Unfortunately the spectacle changes every instant; it is a bewildering kaleidoscope; one does not even know what sort of weather is to be found on this ocean.

Pierre Lalo, who had been so bitter in his earlier criticisms of the young composer, conceded a certain merit to *Miroirs*. Writing of the parts called *Une Barque sur l'océan* and *La Vallée des cloches*, he said: "They are more than exquisite musical diversions . . . they contain sentiment and emotion, beginning to manifest themselves." [4] A number of critics spoke of the originality of Ravel's new suite and said that *Miroirs* marked the beginning of a new type of piano music.

It is not surprising that Ravel, who was unusually sensitive to the beauty of poetry, should have been inspired by the intellectual atmosphere of the Société des Apaches to try his own hand at literature. In 1905 he wrote a charming poem called "Le Noël des jouets" and set it to music as a song dedicated to Mme Cruppi:

> *Le troupeau verni des moutons*
> *Roule en tumulte vers la crèche,*
> *Les lapins tambours brefs et rêches*
> *Couvrent leurs aigres mirlitons.*
>
> *Vierge Marie en crinoline,*
> *Ses yeux d'émail sans cesse ouverts,*
> *En attendant Bonhomme hiver,*
> *Veille Jésus qui se dodine,*
>
> *Car près de là sous un sapin,*
> *Furtif, enveloppé dans l'ombre*
> *Du bois, Belzébuth, le chien sombre,*
> *Guette l'Enfant de sucre peint.*
>
> *Mais les beaux anges incassables*
> *Suspendus par des fils d'archal*
> *Du haut de l'arbuste hiémal*
> *Assurent la paix des étables.*

Et leur vol de clinquant vermeil
Qui cliquette en bruit symétrique
S'accorde au bétail mécanique
Dont la voix grêle bêle: "Noël, Noël!"

The music interprets the fantasy of the poem in delightful fashion, and the deep tones that describe "Beelzebub, the dog of darkness," recall later passages in *Ma Mère l'Oye*. Although not so well known as many others of Ravel's works, it is interesting in its revelation of the childlike quality of his character and in the charming way he uses his art to interpret this.

During this same period also appeared the *Sonatine* for piano, one of Ravel's most sensitive compositions, entered in a contest sponsored by a music periodical of Paris. It is in classical Sonata form, the first movement slow and somewhat melancholy in mood, the second a minuet of great tenderness, and the third a brilliant conclusion. "It is stamped," says Roland-Manuel, "with the double seal of youth and mastery."

These years of association with the most intelligent of the younger generation undoubtedly played a large part in the development of Ravel's general style and character, and in the keen, ironical manner of his art. The friendship and appreciation of the Apaches stimulated him during this period to a creative output which was never equaled in the later years of his career.

LES APACHES

Tristan Klingsor, in his collection of poems called *Humoresques,* mentions with affection his comrade of Apache days:

Jeux d'Eau

Les jeux d'eau dans le parc et la ribambelle
Des fous,
Le cœur troublé des belles
Et le cœur ironique et tendre qui bat sous
Le gilet de velours de Maurice Ravel. . . .

VIII

THE MUSIC OF DEBUSSY AND RAVEL

DEBUSSY'S CHARACTER AND PLACE IN MUSI-
CAL HISTORY—IMPRESSIONISM IN FRENCH
MUSIC—DEBUSSY AND RAVEL CONTRASTED
—CHARACTERISTICS OF RAVEL'S MUSIC

ACHILLE-CLAUDE DEBUSSY was a singular char-
acter—*"très exceptionel, très curieux, très solitaire . . ."*
—artistic, sensuous, and imaginative. His music reflected
these qualities and, together with his originality and
complete departure from tradition and accepted forms
of harmony, marked the beginning of a new era in
musical history.

Ravel was constantly accused—at the beginning of
his career, at least—of imitating Debussy. Undoubtedly
the latter proved a vital inspiration to the younger composer's work, but an examination of Debussy's temperament and music will show how completely he really
differed from Ravel.

This "great painter of dreams," as Romain Rolland
called Debussy, showed from his earliest years a tendency to dreamy emotionalism. He was born in St-

Germain, just outside of Paris, in 1862—thirteen years before Maurice Ravel came into the world. His parents kept a china shop (Ravel's ancestors are said to have been manufacturers of porcelain), and the young Achille-Claude received little or no schooling. He was a shy, sensitive child, with a deep feeling for color, and though his father wanted him to go into the navy his own desire ,was to be a painter. His love of color was later translated into a new expression of music: he used the tones of the scale as a painter blends the colors on his palette.

When he was eight years old Achille-Claude (he later dropped the first name) was given piano lessons by a pupil of Chopin's, who prepared him for the Conservatoire. This he entered at the age of eleven, and two years later won a first medal for *solfège*, though he never went beyond a second prize in piano. He wrote his first composition when he was fourteen—a song called "Nuit d'étoiles"—and this already shows an effort to escape from the bonds of tradition and to find a musical language of his own. It was not until some time later that he developed his own completely individual style, but even in his early years he was constantly experimenting with curious chord progressions and strange harmonizations, and this brought him into disrepute at the Conservatoire.

He is said to have failed in the harmony class because of his persistent use of unorthodox (and hence unpermitted) forms. To those who remonstrated with him he exclaimed: "Why are you so shocked? Are you not able to listen to chords without wishing to know their origin and their destination? . . . What does it matter? Listen; that is sufficient. If you can't make it out, go to Monsieur le Directeur and tell him that I am ruining your ears." [1]

When Debussy was eighteen he won first prize for sight reading at the Conservatoire, and this special gift for reading scores brought him to the attention of Mme von Meck, wealthy Russian patron of music, and "beloved friend" of Tchaikowsky. She engaged the young "de Bussy"—as he then signed his name—to spend the summer with her at the Château de Chenonceaux, to play in a trio which she kept for her special entertainment, and to give lessons to her daughters (with one of whom he fell in love).

"My little pianist, Bussy, is Parisian from tip to toe, a typical *gamin de Paris,* very witty and an excellent mimic. His imitations of Gounod and Ambroise Thomas are perfect and most amusing," Mme von Meck wrote to Tchaikowsky. [2] He spent several summers with the Russian family, and traveled to Switzerland, Italy, and Russia with them.

Debussy was at this time much interested in Wagner, and during the following years visited Bayreuth twice. But the German composer's music gradually lost its attraction: it was too theatrical for Debussy's subtle and less violent nature. Eventually his early admiration for Wagner changed to an antagonism that did much to set him on the quite different path of his own individual style. When he was twenty-nine he made the acquaintance of Erik Satie, and like all the younger musicians of the day was profoundly impressed by Satie's daring originality. (He later orchestrated two of Satie's *Gymnopédies*.)

In 1884 Debussy won the Prix de Rome with his cantata *L'Enfant prodigue*. He had recently lost his heart to Mme Vasnier, the charming young wife of an elderly husband, who had a beautiful voice and sang the youthful composer's songs with gratifying enthusiasm. To her he dedicated "Mandoline" and the first of the *Fêtes galantes*. Debussy spent only two of the prescribed years at the Villa Medici in Rome. He called it a "prison," and thought only of returning to Paris and the Vasniers. *La Damoiselle élue* was the only *Envoi de Rome* that he composed during this period.

From Mme Vasnier, Debussy turned to Gabrielle Dupont. "Gaby of the green eyes" is said to have inspired his celebrated opera *Pelléas et Mélisande*, which was begun at this time, though not completed until ten years later. It was produced in 1902, with Mary Garden and Jean Périer in the title roles, and created the greatest sensation ever known in Paris musical circles. The Apaches admired this opera so extravagantly that they attended every performance *en masse*. Debussy was awarded the cross of the Legion of Honor, and his music became the rage of the day.

In 1899 Debussy married Rosalie Texier, a dress-maker, but soon afterward he deserted "Lily-lo" for Mme Emma Bardac, who became his wife after Rosalie procured a divorce. His only child, "Chou-Chou," was born in 1905; for her he wrote the delightful *Children's Corner* suite for piano. "Chou-Chou" survived her father by a year only.

In addition to his numerous love affairs Debussy had two other passions—cats and the color green. There was always a gray Angora—called Line—to be found in his apartment; in his own nature, too, there was something feline. André Suarèz says: "Just as the cat rubs itself against the hand that strokes it, Debussy caresses his soul with the pleasure he invokes [through his music]."

The year 1909 saw the beginning of the terrible malady which made the last years of the unfortunate Debussy's life a long agony of suffering. He lingered on through the World War, and to his physical pain was added an increasing indignation at the hardships which his country was obliged to endure at the hands of the enemy. He became violently anti-German, and took to signing his name *"Claude Debussy, Musicien français."* He was twice operated for cancer, and died in the midst of the bombardment of Paris, March 25, 1918.

He was the poet of mists and fountains, clouds and rain; of dusk and of glints of sunlight through the leaves; he was moonstruck and seastruck and a lost soul under a sky besprent with stars. All his senses were tributary to his musical inspiration. . . . In transmuting Nature into harmony he has made sonorous his own emotions.[3]

Debussy's music expressed the inevitable revolt against the romanticism of the period just before, and the limitations of too rigid classical forms. He sought escape from these through evolving a style of his own, evanescent and vaporous in its fluidity: the form of music to become known as *impressionism*.

"Impressionism" was a term much in use during the latter part of the last century. It originated with Claude Monet, who exhibited a painting in 1867 called "Impression: Soleil Levant." This "study of light and atmosphere"—an effort to reproduce the sensation of a scene rather than to make a photographic copy of its details— produced a new technique in art. The public, however, did not care for impressionistic paintings. "Unfinished sketches with little or no artistic value" was what it dubbed the work of Monet and his school, and "impressionism" came to be a term of derision.

Closely allied with the impressionist painters were the symbolist poets. They likewise conceived a new interpretation of their art, and saw poetry as an expression of both sound and color. To suggest was their ideal, and while meaning was often sacrificed to effect, they excelled in creating subtle and colorful moods through the musical content of words. When Debussy came upon the scene, music in its turn combined with poetry and painting in a novel blending of sound, color, and emotion.

Stéphane Mallarmé's home was a meeting place for the impressionist painters and poets of the day, and Debussy became an intimate of this circle. It was inevitable that his own tastes should be influenced by and expressed through the ideals of these young artists, and that he should try to follow their principles in his music,[4]

applying their technique to the world of sound, trying to suggest in tone intangible, abstract mental images induced by a thought, an emotion, a perfume, a color, a poem, a scene, any definite object, suppressing unnecessary detail, and reproducing not the reality but the *emotion* evoked by the reality.

Debussy set to music one of Mallarmé's most famous poems: *Prélude à l'après-midi d'un Faune.* Many consider this the finest tone-poem ever written, so perfectly has Debussy captured the mood of delicate sensuousness and the luminous, dreamlike quality of summer haze and pagan delight. Since Manet illustrated the first edition of Mallarmé's poem, *L'Après-midi d'un Faune* may be regarded as a unique embodiment of impressionistic art, through the combined inspiration of leading impressionist poet, painter, and composer.

In *Pelléas et Mélisande* Debussy has created a new form of dramatic music. Instead of successive arias held together by a tissue of orchestral accompaniment, he used the voice in a natural, spoken manner, and through rich and unusual orchestral effects produced an atmosphere of dramatic enchantment—the method that Ravel followed in *L'Heure espagnole.* Of his opera Debussy said:[5]

I have tried to obey a law of beauty which appears to be singularly ignored in dealing with dramatic music. . . . I do not pretend to have discovered everything in *Pelléas*, but I have tried to trace a path that others may follow, broadening it with individual discoveries which will, perhaps, free dramatic music from the heavy yoke under which it has existed for so long.

Debussy's music is essentially "atmosphere"—an evocation of moods, melancholy, voluptuous, or gay as the case may be. In this respect he differs materially from Ravel, who tries to present pictures rather than emotional states. It was due to Ravel's precise and restrained temperament that he developed in a different way from the dreamy Achille-Claude.

In certain respects—mostly minor—the two men resemble each other. Both, for example, used the pentatonic scale *, in writing music in the oriental manner. Both employed certain medieval modes modified by modern harmonization to produce an illusory effect of classic style. The work of both is characterized by paganism, as opposed to traditional religious faith. Finally, there is an interesting similarity between them in their choice of titles.†

The number of parallels in the following list of titles and their remarkable closeness in wording suggests

* The pentatonic scale consists of five notes only, corresponding to the black keys on the piano. It is the scale of primitive peoples, and is still used by the Chinese and the Japanese.

† It is said that Ravel was the first to use descriptive titles instead of the old, conventional tags—prelude, nocturne, valse, etc. But both he and Debussy were probably influenced by Satie in this respect.

how much the two men had in common on this point.

RAVEL	DEBUSSY
Miroirs	Images
Jeux d'eau	Reflets dans l'eau
Rapsodie espagnole	Ibéria
Ma Mère l'Oye	The Children's Corner
Le Tombeau de Couperin	Hommage à Rameau
Menuet sur le nom d'Haydn	Hommage à Haydn

With these similarities, however, the comparison of the two men must end—must yield to their far more striking contrasts. Maurice Ravel was really a classicist, a musical descendant of the older French composers, particularly of Couperin; his clear-cut and carefully planned treatment was in direct antithesis to Debussy's vague, imaginative style. Debussy was a sensualist who expressed his own voluptuous nature in his music— Ravel, an intellectual who had a horror of revealing his feelings and who interpreted only his perception of things. Debussy wrote chiefly in the whole-tone scale, whereas Ravel used the Dorian, Hypodorian, and even the Phrygian modes.

Still more important is the wide divergence between the two in the style and content of their music. Debussy's songs tend toward the erotic, while Ravel's are invariably picture, caricature, or miniature. Ravel's natural idiom lay in ordered rhythm—color and atmosphere *within* form, typically represented by the dance; while Debussy sought to escape from all form, his music being typified by the prelude.

Debussy's music is so highly individual a creation that

95

it became limited by this very personal element; eventually he carried his art to the furthest limits, and exhausted its possibilities. Ravel, on the other hand, escaped this limitation because he never held to any one style: he experimented continuously with new forms, and his music is impersonal and detached.

The two men were as dissimilar in their personal characteristics as in their music. In appearance Debussy was of medium height, with a square body, a large head crowned with a massive forehead, and thick curly hair. He wore a heavy black beard, was inclined to plumpness, and had a swarthy, peculiarly pasty complexion which made some people mistake him for a Syrian. Ravel, on the other hand, was spare and lean, small in stature and fastidious in every detail of his personal life. Whereas Debussy was indolent (in all save his art), Ravel was tireless in his activities. The older composer found inspiration in countless love affairs; Ravel sought his in solitude and in long walks through the country.

Yet in spite of the difference in their natures, Ravel is no less *musicien français* than Debussy. The two composers showed one trait in common (typical of many French people)—their dislike of Wagner and of what they considered the cumbersome musical philosophy of the German school. The reaction against this school of music really began with the Franco-Prussian war. French composers at that time felt that they had been too long under the influence of their German neighbor and must return to a more personal style of their own, in accordance with the earlier tradition of Rameau and Couperin.

National characteristics are nowhere more evident than in music. It is interesting to see how each country has interpreted the soul and temperament of its people through the works of its composers. Germans seek to express emotions, while French musicians have been called "logical sensualists." They are enemies of over-emphasis and ostentation and prefer to describe moods rather than feelings. France is more literary than musical (the ambition of every educated young Frenchman is to write a book!), and its music is therefore more intellectual than emotional and has been, until recently at least, largely an interpretation of poetry through opera and song. Clear and direct, French music seeks simplicity and balance, and is always restrained in its expression.

Ravel has been accused of imitating not only Debussy but other composers as well. To a certain extent this is true; some of his piano numbers were modeled on Liszt and on Chopin; Fauré and Satie furnished the studies for other compositions. As for his orchestral works, it is unquestionable that Ravel found valuable suggestions in the works of Rimsky-Korsakoff, Chabrier, Saint-Saëns, and both Johann and Richard Strauss. He studied the compositions of many besides these, and by all of them was stimulated in his own writing. In this sense he may be said to lack originality.

Is it possible, however, to say what constitutes complete originality? Are not all creations the result of an assimilation of the works of others and of all outside stimuli, plus the individual viewpoint of the artist whose personality transmutes this material into new forms? Anything that stimulates the creative powers of an artist is really legitimate material—provided, of course, that the result is not a direct copy of another's invention.

Ravel, in advising younger composers, said: "Take a model and imitate it. If you have nothing to say, you have nothing better to do than to copy. If you have something to say, your personality will never be more evident than in your unconscious infidelity." This building on or from a pattern is a typical feature of Ravel's music. *"Pastiche,"* the French call it, but a better word would be "transformation." Hoérée says that Ravel's "imitation" makes one forget the model and stamps the borrowed material with the characteristic of the new artisan.[6]

He wishes above all to produce an effect without allowing his labor to be suspected. He avoids appearing in his work. . . . To achieve this he does not try to produce some extraordinary novelty from within himself. It is in imitating that he innovates, for he does not pretend to create *ex nihilo.* He works "on the motif" like a painter. He installs himself before a Mozart sonata or a Saint-Saëns concerto as an artist does before a group of trees. When his work is finished it is usually impossible to find any trace of the model. . . .

Ravel does not dispute with God the privilege of creating his work in his own image. Inheritor of French classics, he follows their example by imitating the ancients. . . .

In Ravel's earlier years he and Debussy were close friends; they shared a common rebellion against tradition, and also an enthusiasm for Mozart, whose compositions they frequently played four-handed. But it was perhaps inevitable that two such individual and outstanding artists should eventually become rivals. An antagonism gradually developed between the two and estranged them completely.

Their esteem for each other as musicians, however, never failed. Ravel dedicated his sonata for violin and cello "To the memory of Claude Debussy" and called him *"le plus considérable, le plus profondément musical des compositeurs d'aujourd'hui."* * He orchestrated Debussy's *Danse* and *Sarabande,* and arranged the *Prélude à l'après-midi d'un Faune* for piano four-hands. This famous tone-poem was Ravel's favorite composition. He often said: *"Je voudrais en mourant entendre* L'Après-midi d'un Faune." †

* "The most eminent, the most profoundly musical of the composers of this age."
† "When I am dying I should like to hear the *Afternoon of a Faun.*"

IX

THE "STORIES FROM NATURE"

EARLY in the new century Ravel made the acquaintance of a young Polish couple, Ida and Cipa Godebski. Cipa, son of a Polish refugee who had come to France in 1831, was crippled as a result of infantile paralysis. His wife was charming, though not beautiful, and their fortune was limited; yet both the Godebskis were so warm-hearted (*si pleins de cœur*) and so genuinely interested in the arts that their apartment became a meeting place for all the young artists of the day.

The *Salon de la rue d'Athènes,* as their drawing-room near the Gare St-Lazare came to be called, had a low ceiling and was so small that, if more than fifteen people gathered there at one time, some had to sit on the floor. But the friendly atmosphere and hospitable welcome made up for all material shortcomings. Ravel, Ricardo Viñes, and Cipa Godebski were all of about the same age, and had many ideas in common. Cipa was a mem-

100

ber of the Apaches, and the group met frequently at his apartment in the rue d'Athènes.

Ravel was diffident in friendship and slow to respond to the advances of others; but once he had given his affection, his loyalty and devotion never changed. Ida and Cipa became his closest friends; in later years, after he moved to the country, he rented a room across the street from the Godebskis so that when he came to Paris he could be close to them and to his great favorites—their two children, Mimie and Jean.

Missia, Cipa Godebski's sister, was married to Alfred Edwards, and in 1905 they invited Ravel to go with them on a cruise on their yacht *Aimée*. He was working at this time on the *Introduction and Allegro for Harp* (with accompaniment of string quartet, flute, and clarinet) which he had promised to the harpist Micheline Kahn, and thought he would hardly be able to finish it before the sailing date; at the last moment, however, he decided to take the manuscript with him and join the Edwardses on their yacht.

With the score under his arm he hurried to the *chemisier* to pick up some gay new shirts he had ordered —for such an important journey required, in Ravel's opinion, an extensive addition to his wardrobe—and dashed down to the boat, only to find that the *Aimée* had sailed without him! He was crestfallen at this disappointment; fortunately, however, he found that he could still reach the yacht a little farther down the river, at Soissons. On his way he discovered that he had left

his precious score in the shop. The *chemisier,* who was
an amateur musician, had carried the manuscript home
and was with difficulty persuaded to relinquish it. But
Ravel, writing to Maurice Delage the following day,
does not even mention the incident. He is all enthusiasm
over the journey: *"La joie de cette journée, mon vieux!"*
Delage says: "This heedlessness and scorn of time created endless difficulties for his good geniuses; they [the
Godebskis] were to find many other manuscripts mislaid
by this man who was in most things so meticulous. . . ." [1]
And Delage quotes this letter: [2]

June 24, 1905

In dry-dock at the port of Amsterdam. We have been here
for three days, and I have not yet visited the Museums. There
are so many things to see! Yesterday, excursion to Harlem.
Some Franz Hals which are a revelation. On the way a magnificent spectacle: a lake bordered with windmills. In the
fields windmills as far as the horizon. Whichever way you
look, you see nothing but revolving wings, and you end by
feeling that you yourself are an automaton in the midst of a
mechanical landscape.

With all this, I do not need to tell you that I am good for
nothing. But I am storing up, and I think a lot of things will
come from this voyage.

While Ravel was in Holland, his family moved to
Levallois-Perret, on the outskirts of Paris. Here the elder
Ravel built a small factory for the production of automobile and machine parts. He was still interested in invention, and had recently designed an automobile which
could perform miraculous somersaults. They called it

the *saut-de-mort,* and in 1903, Joseph and his son Edouard took this invention to the United States, where they exhibited it in Barnum and Bailey's circus. The "jump of death" was performed by a small car (driven by a Frenchman from Paris who went over with the Ravels) which went down a steep track, jumped off into the air, made a complete loop, came down on a continuation of the track and ended up at the bottom. But the career of this invention was ended by an unfortunate accident which took the life of its driver.

Levallois-Perret was an industrial center, where wagons and trucks rolled by in a constant stream. Maurice Ravel did not find much peace or quiet for his work; on the other hand, only a bridge separated him from the open country, and he often walked through the fields or stopped to watch the struttings of the barnyard fowls in the Ferme de l'Etoile just across the way. From his window he could see swans floating in a pond of the farm, and peacocks that raised gorgeous tails and lifted their voices in raucous cries.

Life came to Ravel in terms of music. When at this time he discovered Jules Renard's poems about the peacock and the cricket, the swan, the kingfisher, and the guinea-hen, he set them to a series of inimitable songs. No one but Ravel would have chosen such curiously unmusical subjects. The dry, caustic humor of the poems appealed to his irony-loving temperament, and he interpreted Renard's verses in a unique and highly effective

103

manner, passing with masterly abruptness from mocking humor to the most tender emotion. In these songs Ravel shows his genius for fitting the musical accompaniment to the spoken word. Each inflection of the text is reproduced in a lyrical recitatif which is expressive and never monotonous.

The first of the "Histoires naturelles" ("Le Paon") tells of the solemn and majestic peacock. He is about to be married; but alas, his fiancée does not come. With a strident cry which Ravel interprets to the accompaniment of upward glissandos, the peacock lifts its tail— "like a gorgeous fan heavy with eyes"—and struts pompously away.

"Le Grillon" is a marvel of delicate orchestral mechanics; the vibrating strings create an impression of a quiet landscape by moonlight. The cricket, weary of wandering, returns from his travels and sets his small domain in order. Then he winds up his minute timepiece. ("Has he finished? Is it broken?") Finally he enters his retreat and turns the key in the tiny lock of his door. He listens . . . all is still. . . .

Dans la campagne muette les peupliers se dressent comme des doigts en l'air et désignent la lune.

In the next song, the swan floats serenely on the water watching the reflection of the clouds. But he is not interested in clouds. . . . With a sudden transition of sharp, abrupt chords, he dives to the bottom of the pond, where he "digs with his beak in the nourishing mud and grows

104

e to Ravel's country villa, Le Belvédère, at Montfort-l'Amaury

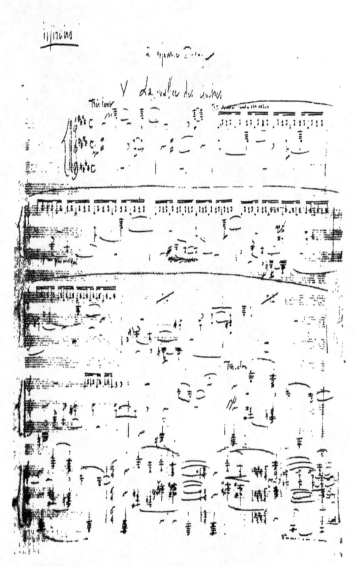

Reproduction of one of Ravel's scores: "La vallée des cloches" from the piano suite *Miroirs*, dedicated to Maurice Delage

as fat as a goose." "Le Cygne" is a masterly take-off on romantic sentimentalism.

"Le Martin-Pêcheur" is the most melodic of the group, filled with gentle melancholy and the plaintive cry of birds at evening. Last comes "La Pintade," malicious hunchback of the barnyard, who always imagines someone is laughing at her. Ravel gives a graphic picture, filled with musical irony, of the shrill-voiced, ridiculous guinea-hen:

Elle se bât sans motif, peutêtre parce qu'elle s'imagine toujours qu'on se moque de sa taille, de son crâne chauve et de sa queue basse.
*Et elle ne cesse de jeter un cri discordant qui perce l'air comme une pointe.**

When Ravel finished his work on the "Stories from Nature" he asked the poet to hear his interpretation. Renard wrote in his diary on January 12, 1907: [3]

M. Ravel, the rich and fastidious composer of "Histoires naturelles," insisted that I should come and hear his melodies this evening. I admitted my ignorance of music and asked what he had been able to add to the "Histoires naturelles" [that is, the poems].
"My intention was not to add, but to interpret."
"But in what way?
"To say with music what you say with words when, for example, you describe a tree. I think and feel in music, and I should like to think and feel the same things that you do.

* She fights motivelessly, perhaps because she keeps imagining that her size is being laughed at, and her bald pate, and her low tail. And endlessly she cries a shrill note that stabs the air like a barb.

There is music that is instinctive, sentimental—my own; of course one must first know one's *métier*, and the music of the intellect. . . ."

When the "Histoires naturelles" were presented to the public in 1907, the audience hardly knew what to make of Ravel's curious treatment of these songs. At first the people were amused, but finally they became outraged. *"Ca n'a pas mordu ce soir,"* sang Mme Bathori, *"mais je rapporte une rare émotion."*

In this work Ravel departed radically from accepted musical interpretation, and thus antagonized those with whom tradition outweighed any novelty, however subtle and effective. The critics attacked him from every side. He was accused of creating a composition as "labored and unmusical" as the text he followed. Lalo called it "a collection of laboriously rarefied harmonies—a succession of involved and complicated chords." He even said it made him think of a music-hall (*"le café-concert avec des neuvièmes"*).

A few, however, defended the young composer. "His special gift," said Henri Ghéon,[4] "is to transmute into music the most unmusical subjects." When Ravel was accused of plagiarizing Debussy a heated argument ensued, for this was a most unjust criticism: nothing could be further removed from Debussy's style than "Histoires naturelles." So hot was the controversy thus aroused that the newspapers seized on the situation and made of it another *affaire Ravel.*

Ravel himself as usual took no part in these arguments. He seemed, all through his life, indifferent alike to praise and to censure, and thought only of escaping from both. As soon as one composition was finished he left it to its fate and turned his attention to a new one. His only interest was in music itself and in experimenting with new forms. He was never content to settle down to one style of writing, but was always eager to try something new, in a different manner. The more intricate the problem to be solved, the better he liked it and the more brilliant his solution. He never chose the easy way; indeed, many of his works contain technical difficulties which seem to be included for the sheer satisfaction of proving their performance possible.

Though the total number of Ravel's compositions is probably less than that of any other composer of equal standing, his works assume greater importance in proportion to their number because of the perfection of each of them. He never considered a composition finished until he had polished every detail to the utmost and was sure that it could stand the severest scrutiny from every angle.

His published songs—only about three dozen in number—include during the first decade of the twentieth century (in addition to "Noël des jouets," "Shéhérazade," and "Histoires naturelles"): "Le Manteau des fleurs" (written in 1903, words by Gravollet), which was later orchestrated; "Les Grands Vents venus d'outremer" (1906, words by H. de Régnier); and in 1907

"Vocalise en forme d'Habanera" and "Sur l'herbe" (words by Verlaine). In this last song Ravel for the first time uses a musical phrase suggestive of the jazz rhythms which interested him so much in later years. "Sur l'herbe" sings of an old Abbé who imbibes too freely of the wine of Cyprus. The song, in minuet style with an incongruous dash of ultramodern harmonization, is like an elegant parody of eighteenth-century gallantry:

> *Ce vin de Chypre est exquis . . .*
> *Que je meure, Mesdames, si*
> *Je ne vous décroche une étoile*
> *Je voudrais être.petit chien!*
> *Embrassons nos bergères, l'une*
> *Après l'autre*
> *Messieurs, eh bien?*
> *Do, mi, sol,*
> *Hé! bonsoir la lune!*

In 1908 Ravel's friend Calvocoressi asked him to harmonize five Greek melodies from a group of popular songs which the latter had collected in Greece, had translated, and now wished to use in illustrating a lecture he was to give at the Sorbonne. There was much in the Greek temperament and tradition which appealed to Ravel. He liked the classical lines and aristocratic paganism of the Hellenic civilization, and a certain ironic restraint manifest in the Greek tragedies found a response in his own reaction against excess. The inspiration of Greece is evident in a number of Ravel's compositions

108

—notably in *Daphnis and Chloe;* though here, as in all his works, the original pattern is completely transformed in the finished product.

Ravel was constantly striving to enlarge and extend the limits of music. Folk-themes appealed to him because they were a natural expression as opposed to the formalized interpretation of the conventional style.

Of the "Five Popular Grecian Melodies," the first is the "Le réveil de la mariée," gay and sprightly; then "Là-bas vers l'église" in slower tempo; "Quel galant!" in which the voice of the singer and the accompaniment answer each other; the "Chanson des cueilleuses de lentisques"; and finally the dancing refrain of "Tout gai!" At the request of Mme Marguerite Babaian, a sixth Grecian melody was added in 1909—"Tripatos"; but this still remains in manuscript form.

The success of the "Cinq mélodies populaires grecques" encouraged Ravel in 1910 to enter a contest sponsored by the Maison du Lied of Moscow for the harmonization of folk-songs of various countries. He wrote seven songs on popular themes of France, Italy, Spain, Scotland, Flanders, Russia, and the Hebrews, and won four out of the ten prizes offered—the French, Italian, Hebrew, and Spanish.

Each of Ravel's songs—each of his compositions, in fact—is distinct and different in style from every other, for he never repeats himself. Yet charming and graphic though his songs are, and brilliant and unusual his piano pieces, Ravel's greatest contribution to music is his amazing genius in orchestration.

All who know Ravel's work marvel at the rich and colorful texture of his orchestration, which has been called "a magic forest whose every tree imprisons a fairy," "a theater in which the instruments become actors."

The orchestra, to Ravel, was like a fascinating piece of machinery. He analyzed and studied its various parts and combinations in much the same way that he delighted in pulling a mechanical toy to pieces to see just how it worked. He explored the deepest possibilities of each instrument—questioned the wood-wind players, the horns, strings, percussions, to find out exactly what tone-effects they were capable of producing. Through the knowledge thus obtained, he was able to create amazing combinations of rare and unusual effects.

Ravel came at a time when everything seemed already to have been said orchestrally. The world was still marveling at the vast musical canvases of Wagner. The Russians, with their brilliant and seductive orchestrations, had captivated everyone; Debussy had recently created impressionism, and Stravinsky was experimenting with new and dynamic harmonizations.

Yet Ravel's orchestration is different from all of these; it is completely and unmistakably his own. Although he learned much from the Russians, from his countrymen Berlioz, Chabrier, and Saint-Saëns, and

110

from Johann and Richard Strauss, Ravel's orchestra does not resemble any of these. It is richer—if less abundant —and more brilliant, luminous, and incisive; organized and intelligent, it is essentially French in its restraint.

True, he made use of certain formulas that had already been discovered by his forerunners; but even these were transformed through his genius into something new and entirely personal. He labored over each page and passage with infinite patience and untiring effort. His completed scores are a miracle of perfection and clearness, capable of withstanding the most severe criticism.

Jean Marnold wrote: [5]

Monsieur Maurice Ravel has created an orchestral language which belongs exclusively to himself. Its extreme subtlety seems by its style to achieve simplicity through a natural unfolding of the infinite resources of each instrument. The basis of this complete mastery is his adequate and profound understanding of these resources.

Ravel thought orchestrally, and he enjoyed this part of his work more than any other. *"C'est un amusement pour moi plûtot qu'un travail,"* he confessed. Many of his compositions which were originally written for the piano (notably *Ma Mère l'Oye* and *Le Tombeau de Couperin*) he later orchestrated.

Besides these, he transcribed for orchestra the following works by other composers:

Debussy—*L'Après-midi d'un Faune; Sarabande; Danse*

Satie—Prelude to *Le Fils des étoiles* (unpublished)

Chopin—*Nocturne, Etude, Valse* (unpublished)

Schumann—*Carnival* (unpublished)

Chabrier—*Menuet pompeux*

Moussorgsky—*Khovantchina* (in collaboration with Stravinsky—unpublished) and *Pictures at an Exhibition*

The best-known of Ravel's arrangements is his famous orchestration of Moussorgsky's *Pictures at an Exhibition*. This suite, with its "Promenade" theme suggesting a spectator walking about from one to the other among canvases exhibited by the painter Hartmann, is a vivid and uniquely brilliant tone-picture. Vuillermoz writes: [6]

One does not have the impression of being in the presence of a second-hand work. The instruments that the orchestrator chooses to translate such and such a design are so perfectly adapted to their function that it is impossible to conceive the text in any other than the sonorous form. In *Pictures at an Exhibition* Ravel has done the work of creator as much as adapter.

Ravel's guides in orchestrating were, first, the *Technique de l'orchestre moderne* by Charles-Marie Widor, and then the concertos of Saint-Saëns and the symphonic poems of Richard Strauss. He orchestrated at the piano, passing constantly from that instrument to his desk and back again, for he declared that only in this way could he hear and isolate the various instrumental groups.

There is little or no similarity between the orchestration of Debussy and that of Ravel. Debussy's is soft, silky, and vaporous, while Ravel's has much more vigor

112

and rhythmic power. The conductor who presents Debussy's works must have unusual sensitivity and feeling; according to his mood he will find different ways of rendering these compositions. But there is only one way of interpreting Ravel's music—and this is especially true of *Bolero*. He leaves nothing to chance; every indication is given on his scores, and it is not possible to add anything or to subtract a note. Only "respectful attention" is required.

Both Debussy and Ravel, however, show a definite reaction against the heavy orchestration of Wagner and the German school. "Wagner used too many instruments for too limited an effect," said Ravel, and his orchestration, like Debussy's, strives to liberate the different instruments and give to each one a definite place and opportunity to be heard. Debussy and Ravel together created a new and typically "French style of dazzling magnificence . . . supple enough to triumph in grandiose evocations as well as in the mysteries of the infinitely small." [7]

X

THE LURE OF SPAIN

RAVEL'S AFFINITY WITH THE SPANISH —"RAP-
SODIE ESPAGNOLE"—DEATH OF RAVEL'S FATHER
—"L'HEURE ESPAGNOLE"—CRITICS' COMMENTS

SPAIN, with its wealth of dance and folk music, was
very close to the heart of Maurice Ravel. His earliest
recollections were centered about the melodies of the
Basque coast, and Spanish rhythms were a part of his
natural heritage. He was, said Manuel de Falla, "more
Spanish than the Spanish themselves"; André Suarèz
called him "un Grec d'Espagne." [1]

I recognize Spain all through Ravel, in what he is as well
as in what he does. This little man so quaint, nervous, slender,
yet unyielding; that cajoling rigidity with the suppleness of
laminated steel; that great nose, those sunken cheeks, that
angular, slim form; his manner a little distant but so courteous; refined in appearance, abrupt in behavior, yet without
incivility; restricted gestures; warmth of embers which forbid
themselves to flare up—this is the Spanish *grillon* [cricket].

The music of Spain has always held a great fascina-
tion for French composers. Bizet's *Carmen,* Chabrier's
España (admiration of Ravel's youth), and Debussy's
Ibéria, all bear witness to the close affinity between the

114

French and the Spanish temperaments. Now Ravel, in 1907, was to add two more important compositions to this list: *Rapsodie espagnole* and *L'Heure espagnole*.

He had always wished to compose an orchestral work based on the folk themes of Spain. One of his first compositions, the *Habanera,* was written in typical Spanish idiom, and since it had never been published he decided to orchestrate and include it in a suite to be called *Rapsodie espagnole.*

Ravel began this work in the summer of 1907, hoping to complete it in time for the fall concerts. But it proved the most difficult as well as the most important undertaking he had so far attempted, and he found it was not easy to concentrate on this work in the crowded Paris apartment which he shared with his parents and his brother Edouard. The Godebskis suggested that he move down to their yacht *Aimée*—which was standing idle, moored to the dock at Valvins near their summer home, "La Grangette"—and live there while working on the new composition. "Here," they told him, "you can be completely protected from interruption."

Ravel took advantage of this offer; in August, 1907, he installed himself on board the *Aimée* and began *Rapsodie espagnole.* Only the captain (*"capable de lui servir une fricassée à l'occasion"*) shared his solitude, and thanks to the quiet of his surroundings he was able to work with intense industry, and completed the suite in a month's time.

Rapsodie espagnole is in four parts: *Prélude à la*

nuit, Malagueña, Habanera, and *Feria.* The first number
is a poem of quiet contemplation, with an opening theme
of four notes, sung by the strings muted, against the
wood winds:

This continues with ceaseless repetition, invoking the
mystery of a languid summer's night.

In *Malagueña* a rhythmic dance slowly develops from
the theme of the *Prélude* and with a chromatic crescendo
works up to a colorful ending. *Malagueña* was especially
well received on its first presentation, and the audience
encored it several times.

Habanera, the third number of *Rapsodie espagnole,*
has been called "a masterpiece of balanced rhythm." It
remains, in its essential form, just as Ravel wrote it in
1895, when he was barely twenty years old. Only the
remarkable orchestration shows his later development.

Feria is in vivid contrast to the three preceding numbers. It is a turbulent dance, full of the *joie de vivre* of
an emotional people—a strange Spanish mixture of
languor and fury which, at the end, mounts to a frenzied
climax. Even in this climax, however, there is an effect
of restraint. Ravel always remains self-controlled, but
leaves the impression that he has deep reserves of emotion which he could draw upon if he wished.

Rapsodie espagnole is essentially an orchestral study.

Here for the first time the full power and color of Ravel's orchestration is in dazzling evidence. Subtle and penetrating contrasts: crescendos of breath-taking intensity, pianissimos faint as a whisper, wild dance rhythms, and heavy lethargy follow each other in bewildering succession. Jean Marnold called the suite "a *féerie* of new and seductive sonorities whose rich luxuriance underlines the slender dimensions of the pieces," [2] and said that it contained enough material to instrument three symphonies.

The *Spanish Rhapsody* was criticized by many for its vague outlines and lack of form. But Jacques Rivière found a rare charm in "the warm sonorous mist" of its "agitation within torpor": [3]

We must understand that the express virtue of this music lies in its very indistinctness; in its dim, floating harmonies; in its perpetual suspense; in its effect of an atmosphere in which everything evaporates.

When *Rapsodie espagnole* was performed by the Colonne Concerts (*"Les Grands Concerts du Dimanche"*) in 1908, the Apaches and others of Ravel's friends attended en masse to applaud their comrade's new suite. The audience as a whole showed appreciation, and called for an encore of the second number; but the *fauteuils d'orchestre*, where the more conservative listeners were seated, appeared less interested. Noting this, Florent Schmitt—member of the Apache clan, winner of the Prix de Rome in 1900, and one of the most gifted of the younger composers—called loudly down from the gallery: *"Encore une fois, pour ceux d'en bas qui n'ont pas compris!"*

There were others who "did not understand." Ravel was accused of affectation, of lacking in abandon, of being too pedantic and too calculating. Still, as a whole, *Rapsodie espagnole* achieved better success than most of his previous works, and today, accustomed as we are to "impressionism" and dissonance in music, this suite of Ravel's seems conservative rather than startling in form.

Ravel took pleasure and even pride in astounding the musical world of his day with his bold harmonizations. He liked to be considered one of the *avant-garde* group— a little ahead of his time in the temerity of his musical speech. When, following the War, a number of young musicians (including the *Groupe des Six*) took over the lead with even more audacious combinations than his own, Ravel was chagrined to find that he no longer belonged in the front ranks of the moderns.

After the move to Levallois-Perret, Joseph Ravel began to fail in health. He complained of serious headaches and lost all his earlier enthusiasm and energy.* Maurice, whose family meant more to him than anything else in life, was seriously concerned over his father's

* Some who knew Joseph Ravel believe that he may have suffered from the same disease of the brain which later took the life of his illustrious son.

condition; in order to please him, and to distract him from his ill health, he now decided to compose an opera. Joseph Ravel adored the theater, and it would have meant much to him to see a work of his own son presented on the stage. He took the greatest pride in Maurice's achievements, and had always hoped that one day he would write an opera.

Ravel's first project was based on Gerhart Hauptmann's famous legend-drama, *The Sunken Bell*. All legend and poetry appealed to the young French composer, but when these included a mechanical setting (such as the foundry in Hauptmann's tale) they proved irresistibly attractive. Ferdinand Hérold, who translated *Die versunkene Glocke* into French and who collaborated with Ravel in cutting and simplifying the cumbersome German text, wrote: [4]

Ravel did not see [in this scene of the foundry] the small workshop of a craftsman; he dreamed of a vast factory, equipped in elaborate fashion like those of today, and he would have used [i.e., set to music] the innumerable sounds of hammers, saws, files, and sirens.

During an unusually hot June at Levallois-Perret, Ravel worked strenuously at the new project. [5]

For two weeks now I haven't left the grind. Never have I worked with such frenzy. Yes—in Compiègne, but there it was less amusing. It is thrilling to do a work for the theater. I won't say it comes all by itself, but that's exactly the best part of it. . . .

In August of the same summer Maurice finally decided to take his father to Switzerland, hoping that the cooler climate and familiar scenes of Joseph's youth would restore him to better health and spirits. From Switzerland Ravel wrote to his friend Delage: [6]

Hermance, 20 August, 1906

So here I am installed in Switzerland, old man, and I no longer regret the ocean so much. . . . It is especially this bland climate, of a surprising purity. My father finds himself rejuvenated, and claims he has hardly any more headaches.

The inhabitants are very curious too. A cousin whom I left a clockmaker is now first violin at the theater in Geneva.

I am awaiting a piano to get back to *The Bell*, momentarily interrupted. . . . Just think, there is already—in addition to what you know of the first act—a large part of the second.

But *The Sunken Bell* was destined never to be completed, for the following spring Ravel discovered a curious one-act play by the French poet Franc-Nohain, and was so captivated by the clocks and the music-boxes of *L'Heure espagnole* that he laid aside the former work and never took it up again (though some of its themes were later used in *L'Enfant et les sortilèges*).

When Ravel had finished *L'Heure espagnole* he took it to Franc-Nohain in order to play the score through, as is customary, for the author's approval, himself humming the vocal parts in the usual inadequate composer's voice. After he had finished playing he waited hopefully for Franc-Nohain's comments. But the latter was not gifted with musical imagination; there was only silence.

120

Le Belvédère from the garden

Edouard Ravel with M. and Mme Bonnet on the balcony of Le Belvé

. . . Finally Franc-Nohain pulled his watch from his pocket: "Fifty-six minutes," he said politely.[7]

Albert Carré, director of the Opéra-Comique, agreed to produce Ravel's opera. But there were difficulties and delays, and although *L'Heure espagnole* was completed in four months' time, it was not until years later—in 1911—that it was given its first performance.

Meanwhile Joseph Ravel's condition grew steadily worse, and on October 13, 1908, he passed away at Levallois-Perret. Maurice was inconsolable, and for many months he could not resume his work. During the year following his father's death he wrote only one composition: *Menuet sur le nom d'Haydn* (for piano).

Ravel called *L'Heure espagnole* a "conversation in music." It is completely different in form from the classical opera, containing few if any of the traditional arias, choruses, and orchestral interludes, and recalling rather the old Italian *opera-buffa*—comedy which is close to farce and at times approaches caricature. It is really an opera in miniature, where the characters resemble marionettes, and everything is compressed into the smallest possible space. The orchestra remains in the background throughout the opera, and the vocal parts are written in such a way that they seem to be spoken rather than sung —*récitatif quasi parlando*. The resulting effect is as natural and unforced as that of an ordinary play or drama, yet more vivid and colorful because of the musical

121

accompaniment which enhances the general effect without ever obtruding.

The scene is laid in a clockmaker's shop in Toledo, Spain, during the eighteenth century. Ravel has so perfectly expressed the mechanical voices of the various timepieces and musical toys that these seem even more alive than the human characters. As has been suggested, it was probably the opportunity to interpret such things in music that led him to choose Franc-Nohain's comedy, for certainly the general tone of the libretto is far removed from his usual fastidious taste. Although inclined to irony Ravel was always *très correct* in morals as well as in personality, and the subtle satire of *L'Heure espagnole* probably appealed more to him than the frankly ribald subject matter of the play.

The overture, or opening prelude, is an enchantingly descriptive piece of musical writing. Emile Vuillermoz calls it "a chorus of little voices of the clocks," "a delicious prelude from which comes the harmonious exhalation of the singing soul of familiar things, where . . . the poetic and remote mystery of minute steel mechanisms is evident." [8]

Even without the stage-setting before our eyes, we can see and feel, in this *Prélude*, the interior of Torquemada's store. Slowly and softly the sounds of the little shop begin to make themselves heard—the tick-tock of the clocks (like quiet breathing), the swinging of their pendulums and the chiming of bells and music-boxes, and finally the voices of Torquemada and Ramiro, the muleteer, who has brought his watch to be repaired. ("It is a family heirloom. My uncle, the toreador, was saved by it from the deadly horns." [9])

Concepcion, the clockmaker's wife, enters, delighted because this is the day when her husband must go out to regulate the government clocks, and she will be free to do as she pleases. But what of Ramiro? Torquemada, in a hurry to be off, asks the muleteer to stay until his return. "Just my luck!" sighs Concepcion. "The one day of the week when my husband is away—the one day when I am free—and I must see it ruined by this stupid man!" (For she is expecting a visit from her lover, the poet Gonzalve.) What shall she do? Perhaps Ramiro can be put to use. . . .

"This clock, Monsieur," she asks him; "in your opinion would it be hard to move? Do you think it would take two men, or three?"

Ramiro, who has more brawn than brain, is delighted to prove his strength. "That clock, Madame? A mere straw, weighing no more than a nutshell! I can lift it easily with one finger." And as he disappears upstairs to put the clock in Concepcion's room, Gonzalve arrives.

There follows an amusing succession of ups and downs with the large Catalan and Normandy clocks. For when Ramiro comes downstairs, Concepcion says she has changed her mind and wants the *other* clock taken to her room instead. Meanwhile she has hidden Gonzalve inside it. The muscular muleteer, little guessing why the clock is so heavy, carries it off upstairs.

While he is gone, another lover appears, the pompous and influential Don Inigo Gomez. ("Because of my position and my great influence, I had your happy husband appointed to care for the government clocks. For it is proper that a husband should have a regular occupation that will take him away from home.")

With two lovers in the house, Concepcion is at her wits' end. When she goes upstairs to pacify Gonzalve inside *his* clock, Inigo, to tease her, conceals himself in the other one and in a falsetto which he imagines to be mechanical imitates the noise of the pendulum and the voice of the cuckoo.

The turbulent Concepcion, however, finds Gonzalve too much interested in composing verses. "Monsieur! Ah, Monsieur!" she cries, running down to Ramiro. "How *can* you expect me to have in my room a clock that will not keep the right time? What a dreadful strain on my nerves!"

While Ramiro, nothing daunted, goes up to bring down the clock with Gonzalve concealed inside, Inigo pleads with Concepcion: "Perhaps you object to my lack of youth and of romance? But being too young has its disadvantages also—a young man is often inexperienced!"

To which Concepcion replies: "Only too true! Only too true!"

On his return with the first clock Ramiro takes it for granted that his fair hostess desires the other in its place. "How about it? Is this other one the clock you want in your room?" Concepcion quickly decides. "Take it—but isn't it too heavy?"

Ramiro, lifting the clock on his shoulders: "Drop of water, grain of sand."

Concepcion regards him with admiration as he carries upstairs the clock—and the corpulent Inigo.

Gonzalve, left alone in his clock, composes a sonnet to the hamadryad of his retreat, but is interrupted by the return of Ramiro, and shortly after by Concepcion herself, this time in a fine rage. ("Oh, *what* a dreadful adventure! Of two lovers, one has no temperament, and the other is ridiculous.")

"Is the clock still bothering you?" asks the muleteer. "There, there, be calm. I'll bring it down again."

The disappointed lady suddenly becomes conscious of Ramiro's charms. ("What calmness—what poise! . . . Truly, I never have seen biceps like his in all my life. . . .") Very sweetly she asks him: "Will you really go upstairs again?"

"Yes," answers Ramiro; "but tell me—which of the clocks shall I take back?"

"Neither one," Concepcion replies, and exits with the muleteer.

Now the two forsaken lovers, Gonzalve and Inigo, are left alone in the shop, each in his clock, and here the returning Torquemada finds them. "What greater joy for a clockmaker than to return and find many customers waiting in his shop!" he exclaims joyfully, all unconscious of the curious situation. Inigo and Gonzalve, to cover their confusion, feign great interest in their respective clocks, and the shrewd Torquemada takes advantage of their discomfiture by selling them these timepieces at an exorbitant figure.

But the portly Inigo is stuck fast within his narrow box, and Torquemada and Gonzalve together cannot pull him out. Concepcion, returning with Ramiro, makes a chain with the two others—and still Inigo remains tight fast. The muleteer, however, takes him around the waist and lifts him out without the slightest difficulty. . . .

The opera ends with an exquisite quintet—*"un exemple virtuose de l'équilibre vocal"*—all the actors singing together "the moral from Boccaccio":

> *Entre tous les amants, seul amant efficace,*
> *Il arrive un moment, dans les déduits d'amour,*
> *Où le muletier a son tour!* *

On May 19, 1911, *L'Heure espagnole* was presented at the Opéra-Comique along with a little-known opera of Massenet's called *Thérèse*. Again the critics were divided in their opinions. Some could see only the risqué side of the work. They called it a "miniature pornographic vaudeville" and regretted that Ravel should have wasted his talents on such an unworthy subject. They said that he was more interested in imitating the mechanism of clocks than in interpreting his characters' emotions; that the people of the play were like the automatic dolls of

---

* Among lovers the one who's efficient succeeds. In the pursuit of love there arrives a moment when the muleteer has his turn.

a musical clock—without soul or life; that the music "made one think of *Pelléas,* but a *Pelléas* reproduced on a gramophone in very slow motion." [10]

All the critics, however, agreed that the orchestration was delightful and without equal in the art of contemporary music. Lalo [11] compared it to "the orchestral imagination of a Richard Strauss; but of a miniature Strauss, a Strauss who works in the infinitely small . . . An orchestration charming, brilliant, unusual, diverse, full of subtle values and rare sonorities." Vuillermoz wrote: [12] "Ravel creates colors. He is painter, goldsmith, and jeweler."

After the first presentation of *L'Heure espagnole* at the Opéra-Comique, Ravel's friends waited anxiously to hear what his reaction would be to the performance. But Ravel—who, as we have seen, was extremely fastidious in his dress—proved to have but one thing on his mind.

"Did you notice that all the *grand monde* is wearing midnight-blue evening clothes?" he exclaimed. "And to think that after I especially ordered a new blue suit for tonight, that stupid tailor of mine forgot to deliver it!"

XI

MA MÈRE L'OYE

RAVEL AND THE GODEBSKI CHILDREN——"MA MÈRE L'OYE"——THE SOCIÉTÉ MUSICALE INDÉPENDANTE ——ITS CONCERTS CRITICIZED——"GASPARD DE LA NUIT"——RAVEL'S OPINIONS OF OTHER COMPOSERS

"*IL était une fois. . . .*"

Ravel, with little Mimie Godebska on his knee, and Jean on a stool at his feet, sat before the fire in the salon of the rue d'Athènes.

There was something very childlike and ingenuous in Ravel's own character. He adored children and felt completely at home in the company of the younger generation. He invented games for them and told them stories by the hour. For he himself had never left the world of make-believe, and the tales of princesses and fairy gardens were as real to him as to his young friends.

Jean and Mimie, the Godebskis' young children, had known Ravel since babyhood, and they were his close companions. Whenever he had a free moment he would stop in to have a romp with them. Sometimes it was late in the evening, when the servants had finished their work and had already gone to bed.[1]

128

"*Pardon,*" he would exclaim. "I did not realize it was so late!"

"But have you dined, *mon cher Maurice?*"

Ravel, to whom time was of no importance and who could not realize why it should have such value for other people, would reply: "Just give me a bite of anything you happen to have. . . ."

While Mme Godebska went to the kitchen to forage for cold meat and a length of French bread, Mimie and Jean appropriated their friend. He usually brought them some small toy or game. At New Year's the boulevards swarmed with peddlers selling mechanical gimcracks, and Ravel would spend fascinated hours examining and purchasing a collection of these for his young friends. Once, to his delight, he found a small boat in which diminutive Japanese figures rowed and at the same time put out their tongues. To Mme Godebska he brought miniature Japanese gardens and dwarf pines.

Ravel was always ready to amuse the children with new tricks. Sometimes he cut out paper-dolls for them (he was very clever with his hands), or got down on all fours and chased them about the room until Mimie screamed with excitement. The children often took advantage of his good nature ("—but you will spoil them, *mon ami!*—") and teased him unmercifully. He would retaliate by attacking them with pillows, and the fight usually ended in a big armchair before the fire, and a request for a story. Mimie would drowse in his arms,

129

while Jean listened wide-eyed to the familiar tales of Beauty and the Beast, Tom Thumb, and Laideronnette.

"Once upon a time . . ."

Ida and Cipa Godebski began the musical education of their children at an early age. Jean showed a certain talent, but Mimie rebelled against practising. To encourage the two children, their *grand ami barbu* (Ravel wore his black beard at this time) decided to compose some special four-hand music which they could play together. He took five of their favorite stories: Sleeping Beauty, Hop o' my Thumb, Laideronnette, Beauty and the Beast, and The Fairy Garden, and wrote for them a delightful suite called *Ma Mère l'Oye*.

Because of his own childlike nature and poetical imagination, Ravel was singularly well fitted to set the familiar tales to music. Never has he come so close to the heart of childhood as in these simple but exquisite pieces; they are filled with a tenderness rarely to be found in his other compositions. In *Ma Mère l'Oye* he seems to have forgotten the reserve which he ordinarily maintained before the world, and to have opened his heart completely. His usual "artificial" style here gives way to an enchanting simplicity and freshness of inspiration.

First in this fairyland suite comes the *Pavane de la Belle au bois dormant*, in two-voice counterpoint style. This is a slow, short dance (only twenty measures long) of graceful and mysterious charm, completely different

130

in form from Ravel's earlier *Pavane pour une Infante défunte.*

Next follows *Petit Poucet* (Hop o' my Thumb). The story, by Perrault, tells of a poor woodcutter's children abandoned in the forest. On Ravel's score is the following quotation:

He [Petit Poucet] believed that he could easily find his path by means of bread crumbs which he had scattered wherever he passed; but he was very much surprised when he could not find a single crumb: the birds had come and eaten everything up.

The music describes Hop o' my Thumb's despair and the cries of the hungry birds.

Laideronnette, Impératrice des Pagodes is a Chinese scene in miniature, brilliant with the tinkling of crystal bells which form an enchanting background for the tale of the Empress of the Pagodas. Two melodies, the first gay and the second slow, sound alternately and then together.

Laideronnette was taken from a seventeenth-century tale written by the Countess Marie d'Aulnoy called *Serpentin Vert.* In this narrative a beautiful princess is cursed by a wicked fairy and doomed to a life of horrible ugliness. She is well named "ugly one" (Laideronnette) and is so unhappy that she hides herself in a far-away castle. Here she meets a large green serpent (Serpentin Vert) who takes her to sea in a small boat. They are wrecked on the island of the Pagodins—diminutive creatures whose bodies are made of crystal, porcelain, and

131

precious stones. Ravel's music describes the following scene:

> She undressed and got into her bath. Immediately the Pagodas and Pagodins began to sing and play on their instruments. Some had theorbos made of walnut shells; others had viols made of the shell of an almond, for of course it was necessary to fit the instruments to their size.

Laideronnette becomes Empress of the Pagodas, and marries Serpentin Vert, who straightway turns into a handsome young prince, while his bride's beauty is restored—and they "live happily ever after. . . ."

Les entretiens de la Belle et la Bête (from a story by Mme Beaumont) contains a singularly realistic conversation (*mouvement de Valse très modérée*) between the unhappy prince, transformed into a beast, and the compassionate young princess who is a little fearful of the ugly monster. Ravel quotes the two following "discourses" in his music:

> "When I think how good-hearted you are, you do not seem to me so ugly."
> "Yes, I have indeed a kind heart; but I am a monster."
> "There are many men more monstrous than you."
> "If I had wit, I would invent a fine compliment to thank you, but I am only a beast."
>
> .   .   .   .
>
> "Beauty, will you be my wife?"
> "No, Beast!"
> "I die content since I have the pleasure of seeing you again."
> "No, my dear Beast, you shall not die; you shall live to be my husband!"

The Beast had disappeared, and she saw at her feet only a prince more beautiful than Love, who thanked her for having broken his enchantment.

In the orchestration of this number the Beast's deep tones are amusingly interpreted by the bassoon, and the composition ends with his joyous transfiguration as the Princess breaks the spell that binds him. Parts of this work recall Satie's first *Gymnopédie*.

The finale of the suite, marked *lent et grave,* is like a delicate watercolor picturing a magical garden. *Le Jardin Féerique* swells into a pæan of praise to beauty; here Ravel gives full sway to the inspiration of that other world which meant more to him than the actual. He was always, in a sense, trying to escape from reality; he looked at life rather than took part in it, and preferred to create his own world—a subnatural place peopled with fairies and mechanical marvels, where the rude winds of violent emotion never blew. These things inspired him and called to him for interpretation; in setting them to music he felt safe—no one could here accuse him of sentimentalism. He could attack his problem with complete detachment and impersonality.

To some people Ravel's music seems a soulless, brittle thing—delightful, but without depth, and at times touched with malice (*"pince sans rire,"* some have called him). He has even been accused of superficiality, but if this be true then it is the superficiality of one who scorns to show his feelings to the world—whose emotions are

too intense for probing. These feelings nevertheless occasionally break through the mask of indifference with
which he seeks to conceal them, and it is this sense of
hidden depths and restrained emotion that makes Ravel's
music so intriguing and at the same time so delightful.

Mimie and Jean Godebski were too young to appreciate the importance of their friend's gift. Ravel had
hoped that the children would be able to play *Ma Mère
l'Oye* at a public concert. But Mimie was paralyzed at
the thought—stubbornly refused to practise; and they
finally had to abandon the idea.

The original version of *Ma Mère l'Oye* (four-handed
piano) was played by two young pupils of Mme Marguerite Long * (Christine Verger, six years old, and
Germaine Duramy, ten) at the first concert of the Société
Musicale Indépendante in 1910. This Society had been
founded in the spring of that year in opposition to the
Société Nationale de Musique and the Schola Cantorum,
by a group of young musicians who felt that these older
groups were too prejudiced in favor of the classical
school.

Here is an interesting example of the restricting power
of organization. As soon as an idea becomes cast into a
mold it begins to lose the compelling force which
prompted it, until finally the form not only prevents
further growth, but even destroys its own inspiration.

* Well-known soloist and head of the piano department at the
Paris Conservatory.

View of the village from the balcony of Le Belvédère

(*upper*) The writing-table in Ravel's gloomy study, with open window looking out over the Ile de France countryside

(*lower*) Ravel loved toys; "Zizi," the mechanical bird, was his favorite.

The Société Nationale had been founded originally with exactly the same principles as its younger rival, the S.M.I.—i.e., to provide a vehicle for presenting the works of contemporary composers. But gradually the older society lost the liberalism of its early aims and became so conservative that it could see no merit in the music of the younger composers. Most of these, it felt, were "revolutionary" and lacking in that "high artistic aspiration" required in those who were privileged to appear before the Société Nationale. The younger musicians, therefore, decided to create a vehicle of their own, a more tolerant one that would be principally engaged in presenting the music of their immediate generation. Fauré was elected first president of the Society, and Ravel was one of its founders.

While Ravel and a few others were concerned only with sincerely expressing their own individuality in music, many of the younger composers deliberately tried to be original at any cost, and sacrificed all tradition in an effort to escape the commonplace and obvious. Mannerisms took the place of inspiration, and a fear of boredom led these moderns to resort to endless innovations.

The music of this period following Debussy was largely given over to dissonance, typical of the restless questioning spirit of the age. The completed harmonic resolutions of the classical music seemed to the younger composers to indicate immobility—a state incapable of further development; whereas the unresolved chords of

135

dissonance implied growth and expansion into the unknown. Because an opinion or a form was an accepted thing, they distrusted it on principle; but in their search for larger and ever-receding horizons they sometimes lost all touch with common humanity and sacrificed inspiration to mere cleverness.

The Société Musicale Indépendante was not long in achieving notoriety. While its aim to liberate music from the unnecessary restrictions of old traditions was a worthy object, the results did not always prove felicitous, and the average listener could neither understand nor appreciate what the younger composers were trying to express. Some fine programs of sincere and valuable works were presented, but as a whole the criticisms of the conservatives were not entirely unjustified.

The noted American composer and author, Daniel Gregory Mason, has put into a recent book (*Music in My Time*) his impressions of music in Paris during this period, from which the following paragraphs may be quoted: [2]

The maddening thing about the Parisian musical mode at that period was its artificiality, its narrow cliquism, its self-conscious complacency and intolerance, its itch for personal publicity and indifference to any larger beauty. There were of course sincere musicians there—d'Indy, Dukas, Fauré, Florent Schmitt, and within their narrow limits even Debussy and Ravel—but those who made the most noise and succeeded in hypnotizing the world of fashion, after all indifferent to beauty, were the *arrivistes*, the *poseurs*, and the snobs and the bluffers. "We make the fashion and we follow it"—so d'Indy expresses for them their pose—"Let us be little, let us be original." . . .

If one could only have ignored these *arrivistes* with a good conscience, their effect, omnipresent as they were, might have been less depressing; but of course one could only tell by exposing oneself to them how much of real value might be mixed with their pretentious nonsense. So one went to dreary concerts of the *Société Musicale Indépendante*.

The year following the inauguration of the S.M.I., Ravel (as has already been mentioned) organized a concert of Erik Satie's works under the auspices of the new society. At this concert he himself played Satie's *Sarabande*, the *Third Gymnopédie*, the prelude to *Le Fils des étoiles*, and (with Ricardo Viñes) *Pièces en forme de poire*.

From the childlike fantasy of *Ma Mère l'Oye*, Ravel turned to the strange, lugubrious poems of Aloysius Bertrand, and wrote a suite for piano called *Gaspard de la Nuit*. The three numbers that make up this group— *Ondine, Le Gibet,* and *Scarbo*—"sum up all the virtues of Ravel's music and the strength of his genius . . . [they are] heavy with the enchantment of nocturnal visions." [3]

In poetry, as in fairy-tales and folklore, Ravel was particularly attracted by those passages which could be given a musical interpretation. His style is so descriptive that he is exceptionally successful in creating realistic effects. Each of his compositions shows some new or unusually graphic bit of writing. In *Ondine* a new sound-

137

picture of water is produced. Drops fall in a shower of arpeggios, recalling the brilliance of *Jeux d'eau*, though in this composition Ravel uses a quite different form.

Le Gibet evokes a gallows in a mournful landscape; in the distance a deep bell tolls implacably:

C'est la cloche qui tinte aux murs d'une ville sous l'horizon
*Et la carcasse d'un pendu que rougit le soleil couchant.**

The stark simplicity of the music emphasizes the despairing tragedy of the scene. Its restrained emotion has much greater effectiveness than a more dramatic interpretation would have achieved.

Scarbo is a grimacing will-o'-the-wisp, who rolls strangely *"comme le fuseau tombé de la quenouille d'une sorcière"* and is finally blown out "like the flame of a wax taper." This number is a sparkling whirlwind of pianistic virtuosity, in which the ironic Scarbo weaves his way through a scherzo of infernal gaiety and brings the suite to a dazzling conclusion. *Scarbo* is dedicated to the American pianist Rudolph Ganz, while *Ondine* is inscribed to Harold Bauer.

Gaspard de la Nuit marks the summit of Ravel's pianistic art. Alfred Cortot writes of this suite: *

These three poems enrich the piano repertoire of our epoch with one of the most extraordinary examples of instrumental ingenuity which the industry of composers has ever produced.

---

* 'Tis the bell that tolls at the walls of a city beneath the horizon,
  And the corpse of a hanged man reddened by the setting sun.

In an article devoted to a discussion of Ravel's piano music, Henri Gil-Marchex says that Ravel's scores are intricate, but not difficult to follow: [5]

The writing is always admirably clear, every sign having its exact importance; I know no other text that requires an interpretation so carefully following the written indications. The magical formulas are all prepared, with a precision almost hair-splitting; all that is necessary is to read the text with scrupulous care, and no mistake can be made in the pianistic interpretation. On the other hand, the poetic interpretation is most subtle, and the effort of imagination necessary to translate Ravel's thought is far beyond the ability of ordinary players. . . . It is music to be played with the heart, but also with clear intelligence.

Ravel (*"œil clair, dent dure, plume aigüe"*) wrote articles for various newspapers and periodicals, and in these expressed his opinion of a number of his fellow-composers. Liszt, he said, was "a vast and magnificent chaos of musical material from which several generations of illustrious composers have drawn inspiration." *"Heureusement que Wagner avait Liszt,"* he remarked, for to him the latter was the greater musician of the two. Wagner's music he called "a howling flood of pagan life" that "made him feel the need of peaceful, even austere, retreat."

Beethoven (*"le grand sourd"*) appealed to Ravel chiefly because of his quartets. Brahms, he said, had "brilliant orchestral technique, but too much artificiality." *"Ça ne vole jamais, la musique de Brahms . . ."* (It is interesting to note that few French people under-

139

stand Brahms or care for his music, while on the other hand the Germans do not appreciate Fauré.) Among the modern German composers he considered Richard Strauss the greatest, and thought his orchestration a thing of magic. (When he heard *Elektra,* Ravel said he "felt as if his entrails were being ripped out." Although he acknowledged the mastery of this work he hated its brutality and force.)

César Franck's music, while "of an elevated character containing daring harmonies of singular richness" (*"les portes du Paradis qui s'ouvrent"*), seemed to Ravel to be filled with "lamentably frequent repetition and poverty of form."

Bach appealed to Ravel less than did Couperin, but of all composers Mozart was his favorite. *"C'est un dieu,"* he said. "Mozart was not a human being—he was a god."

Ravel's personality and character captured the general public and critics no less than his music. Though many sought to understand his enigmatical temperament and the motives which inspired his work, few were successful. An interesting pen portrait was written by Emile Vuillermoz: [6]

Neither critics nor photographers have ever been able to arrive at any but contradictory and inaccurate portrayals. His audacious nose, thin lips, hermetic mouth, eyes gay and cruel, face in which a wood-engraver has notched the wrinkles too energetically, the profile of his skull which a sculptor has modeled with a daring hand, the severe, parched lines of his thin, mechanical body with its slightly tanned skin like that of a retired sailor—all these form a disconcerting whole.

One sees in him, as a rule, isolated details that do not go well together. He is a child and an old man. A nothing amuses him, and yet his ravaged face often takes on a severe and reserved expression. He passes without transition from childish heedlessness to painful gravity. He often looks as if he were suffering. His tormented features and frowning brow reveal one knows not what dark conflict. . . .

His look of a worried young fox or a mouse scenting traps everywhere is surprising in an artist so lucid, spontaneous, and precise, who has nothing to fear from life. Is he the only one who fails to know the infallibility of his own creative powers? He has never had an unpleasant surprise in putting into play the mechanism which he has patiently and minutely adjusted and geared, like the movement of a clock. He is reproached with fabricating automatic toys; but they are marvelous toys that have a powerful effect on our imagination and on our sensibilities, the magnificent toys of grown-up children.

XII

DAPHNIS AND CHLOE

THE COMTESSE DE ST-MARCEAUX'S SALON
——DIAGHILEFF AND THE BALLET RUSSE——
RAVEL GOES TO LA GRANGETTE TO COM-
POSE A BALLET——"DAPHNIS AND CHLOE"

THE Comtesse de Saint-Marceaux was a woman of
great artistic appreciation; her salon on the Boulevard
Malesherbes had become celebrated throughout Paris,
and an invitation to her soirees was a privilege much to
be desired. Here, during the early years of the new century, all the outstanding personalities of the day could
be found.

On Thursday and Sunday evenings the *grand monde*
of Paris, in full formal attire, filled the salons of the
Hôtel St-Marceaux. But Wednesdays were consecrated
to the artistic world——to writers, painters, and sculptors,
but chiefly to those who were interested in music. In-
formality was the rule; no dress clothes were allowed
(this, in a period of extreme conventionality, was a rev-
olution in itself), and music was the main concern of
the evening. First an excellent dinner was served, and
following this the company adjourned to the drawing-

142

rooms, where shaded lamps, luxurious furnishings, and —most important of all—two Pleyel pianos provided an attractive setting for pleasant and stimulating entertainment.

The music of contemporary composers was more welcomed than that of the "Old Guard"; however, Fauré and Messager sometimes amused the visitors with four-handed parodies of Wagner's operas. "Often," writes Mme Colette in her souvenirs of this period,[1] "side by side on one of the piano benches they improvised four-handed, rivaling each other in *modulations brusquées, évasions hors du ton*. They both loved this game, during which they challenged each other like duelists: '*Pare celle-la! . . . Et celle-la, tu l'attendais?*' . . ."

The guests were not obliged to listen to the music; some of them would perhaps retire to a quiet spot for an argument on the relative merits of the newer composers; others might choose a book from the well-filled library, or amuse themselves with Mme de Saint-Marceaux's diminutive pet *ouistiti* (marmoset), while an artist settled himself in a corner to pencil a surreptitious sketch of one of the celebrities present. But when the music began, a respectful attention was required of everyone.

Monsieur and Madame de Saint-Marceaux were intelligent and delightful hosts; the congenial atmosphere of this home inspired their musical friends to bring new compositions and play these for the discriminating and appreciative audience always to be found there. Many world-renowned works were here heard for the first time.

Messager once arrived with the score of *Pelléas et Mélisande* "clasped to his heart as if he had stolen it. He began to read it at the piano, and to sing it passionately, with a voice of rusted zinc. He would stop, begin again: 'And this! . . . And this!' And when he sang the role of Mélisande his eyes were almost closed. . . ." [2] In later years Falla's *Three-Cornered Hat* was also heard at Mme de Saint-Marceaux's soirees in manuscript form.

Here, one evening, came a slender, meticulously attired young man, whose luxuriant black hair and sweeping moustache made his head seem too large for his slight body. He was dressed in the very latest style; a waistcoat of rich pattern was set off by a carefully tied cravat, and a linen jabot on his immaculate white shirt completed the picture of an elegant precisian. The young man's shy and retiring nature concealed itself behind a distant, almost forbidding manner which at first disconcerted those who did not know him.

But when Maurice Ravel played some of his music, this first impression gradually changed; he soon created an important place for himself at Mme de Saint-Marceaux's soirees, and his audience's sympathetic appreciation helped him to overcome much of his natural reserve. It was not easy, however, to persuade him to play after his first interest in a new composition had worn off; even if it were his own he rarely cared to hear it again. A frequent visitor at the Hôtel Saint-Marceau, he seems to have enjoyed the music itself less than the personal contacts with painters, writers, and other musicians. *"J'aime mieux faire de la musique que de l'entendre,"* he remarked with more truth than humor. *"J'en ai presque tout de suite assez."*

It was not long before Ravel gained a reputation for holding unusual opinions, and this renown delighted his mischief-loving spirit. He was said to be so fond of paradoxes that he could be made to contradict himself for the sake of one. He was always courteous and appreciative of feminine beauty and charm; as a whole, the other sex attracted him, though no single member claimed his exclusive allegiance. Many recall his unusual if scarcely complimentary remark: "I prefer a beautiful locomotive to a beautiful woman! *Au fond,"* he added, *"ma seule maîtresse, c'est la musique."*

In 1909 the Russian Ballet swept into Paris with a dazzling pageant of gorgeous color, frenzied dancing, and music. This new expression of the arts aroused the conservative French people to unparalleled enthusiasm. The sensual charm of the music and glittering confusion and magnificence of the settings made the Ballets Russes the *dernier cri* of all artistic circles. Sergei Diaghileff, organizer of the ballet, became the most popular character of the day.

Diaghileff, said to be the natural son of a Czar, was a man of unusual taste and genius, and to these talents he added an extraordinary ability for organization. During his first season in Paris he gave concerts introducing the Russian composers, and in 1908 produced Moussorgsky's opera *Boris Godunov*, with Chaliapin in the title role. In 1909 he established the Russian Ballet and gathered together a brilliant company which included the painter Bakst, the choreographer Fokine, and such peerless dancers as Nijinsky, Pavlova, Karsavina, and Adolf Bolm. Ida Rubinstein was originally a member of this group.

While Diaghileff interpreted in these ballets the music of his countrymen—Rimsky-Korsakoff's *Scheherazade* and *Coq d'or*, Tchaikowsky's *Nutcracker Suite* and *Belle au bois dormant*, the dances from Borodin's *Prince Igor*, and others—at the same time his restless and inventive nature was constantly seeking for new material, and he soon turned to the younger composers of his day and commissioned them to write for him. In this way he became a patron and inspirer of much that is finest in modern music.

Stravinsky, at this time a struggling and almost unknown composer, was given an order to write a ballet on the Russian fairy-tale of the Fire-Bird. The result was a masterpiece of such powerful originality and harsh dissonance that few people were able to appreciate this strange new music. The fiery young composer—called *"Igor le Terrible"* because of his open rebellion against all that was charming, vague, or traditional—was the cause of endless controversies in the musical world. Hardly anyone could understand what he was trying to say; when *Petrouchka* appeared a year after *L'Oiseau de feu*, some of the critics said that its composer must be mentally unbalanced; the famous *Sacre du printemps*, written in 1913, created a riot at its first presentation. Maurice Ravel, however, was one of the few who from the beginning knew the value of the talented young composer's work. *L'Oiseau de feu* impressed Ravel more than anything he had heard since Chabrier—especially its extraordinary orchestration—and Stravinsky became one of his close and lifelong friends.

Other outstanding successes of Diaghileff's ballet were Debussy's *Prélude à l'après-midi d'un Faune*, danced in inimitable fashion by the great Nijinsky, Strauss's *Till Eulenspiegel*, and Falla's *Three-Cornered Hat*. Their repertoire also included works by Prokofieff and—after the war—by Poulenc, Auric, and Milhaud.

During his first years in Paris Diaghileff heard the music of a young French composer named Maurice Ravel, whose vivid and rhythmical style seemed to him particularly suited to the ballet. In 1910 he asked Ravel to write a ballet on the Greek legend of Daphnis and Chloe.

Ravel was more than pleased by this commission. Here was a medium of expression well suited to the peculiar element of his genius—for the ballet is fundamentally an interpretation of sound made graphic by brilliant stage settings and vivid costumes, and rhythm perfectly visualized through the dance.

The original libretto of *Daphnis and Chloe*, taken from a fable of Longus and arranged by Michel Fokine,

147

choreographer of the group, did not altogether satisfy Ravel. It was inevitable that differences of opinion should arise between the Russians, with their primitive Eastern temperaments, and the highly sophisticated French composer. Ravel had his own ideas, and refused to be a slave to the exigencies of the dancé; he saw the Greek legend of Daphnis and Chloe in a typically eighteenth-century atmosphere of Watteau shepherdesses and the classical paintings of David, while Bakst planned the stage settings in a complete antithesis of bold and gorgeous oriental colorings.

A compromise between the two was eventually arranged. Some changes were made in the libretto, and Ravel set to work on the new composition. At the insistence of his good friends the Godebskis he moved, in March 1910, to their summer home at Valvins, where he could work undisturbed. "La Grangette" was far enough away to be secluded from the visits of casual friends; automobiles were few and far between, and a two-kilometer walk through the forest of Fontainebleau separated "La Grangette" from the nearest railway station. Mimie Godebska—now Mme Blacque-Belair—tells of the whistled signal which announced the occasional approach through the forest of a brother Apache—the old rally-call from Borodin's Second Symphony:

Here in the country Ravel could concentrate in perfect freedom; at his door the beautiful forest of Fontainebleau offered him rest and the inspiration of its leafy roads. Many of the enchanting themes of *Daphnis and Chloe* may have been suggested to him during his long walks through the woods. Trees and forests were a necessity to Maurice Ravel's quiet-loving nature. He later chose his permanent home at the edge of the Rambouillet forest, and the chief joy of his tragic last years was found in solitary rambles through the woods.

While he was at Valvins the Seine overflowed its banks, and the waters rose to the door of the Godebskis' villa. Ravel, intent on his composing, was hardly aware of the flood. Friends who, concerned over his safety, came to see how he was faring, found him quietly working at the piano while the floor beneath the living-room buckled in dangerous fashion from the pressure of the flood waters beneath.

Never was ballet music so carefully prepared and polished as that of *Daphnis and Chloe*. The "Bacchanale" at the close took a year to complete, and, even after it had been finished and was apparently ready for performance, it was *remise sur le métier;* Ravel saw ways to make it still better, and took it back for further polishing.

In spite of the perfection of the music, however, *Daphnis and Chloe* as a ballet was not a complete success. The plot and action are perhaps not sufficiently dramatic to hold the attention of an audience. In addition

to this, and possibly because Ravel was so long in pre-
paring the score, sufficient time was not allowed for the
preparation of the first performance. There was discord
among Diaghileff, Fokine, and Bakst, each having different ideas about the set-up. Nijinsky too had his own
conception as to the way the role of Daphnis should be
interpreted. The chorus had difficulty with their parts,
while the corps de ballet struggled with the curious ⁵⁄₄
rhythm of the Finale.

On June 8, 1912, the first performance was given at
the Châtelet Theater with Pierre Monteux conducting.
Nijinsky and Karsavina danced the title roles, and Adolf
Bolm and Mlle Frohman took the parts of Dorcon and
Lycenion. The settings by Bakst were a startling and
effective riot of colors, though hardly in the spirit of
ancient Greece.

The opening and closing scenes of *Daphnis and Chloe*
take place at the edge of a sacred wood dedicated to the
god Pan and his attendant nymphs. A group of young
Greek maidens and shepherds arrive bringing offerings
of fruits and flowers to place upon the altar. Ravel's
"Introduction et danse religieuse" creates an atmosphere
of pastoral charm and quiet grace. While a sacred dance
is performed in honor of the great god Pan, a chorus
of mixed voices from behind the scenes sings a muted
accompaniment of moving beauty. This chorus was the
object of much controversy between Diaghileff and
Ravel; the former contended that it was unnecessary,
unsuited in register to the voices of average singers, and

150

an added and useless expense to the production. In later performances in England the choruses were omitted, to Ravel's regret and disapproval.

Following the "Danse religieuse" Chloe appears with the shepherd Daphnis, and they are surrounded by a crowd of young people. Dorcon, the cowherd, attempts to embrace Chloe, but he is violently repulsed by Daphnis. A dance contest between the two is suggested with a kiss from Chloe as a recompense. Dorcon's performance is a primitive, robust affair, full of grotesque energy (Adolf Bolm achieved a triumph in his interpretation) and a complete contrast to the graceful, dreamy measures of Chloe's chosen lover.

Chloe, having rewarded Daphnis with a kiss, departs with the maidens, while her lover reclines under a tree. Lycenion, who has remained behind, attempts to seduce him, dropping her veil as she dances in voluptuous measures. Suddenly there is a distant sound of warlike cries and tumult. A band of pirates appears, pursuing the fleeing shepherdesses.

Daphnis, believing Chloe to be among them, dashes after to protect her. But as he disappears she runs in from the other direction and falls exhausted at the foot of the altar, imploring the god's aid. The pirates find her there and carry her away. Daphnis, returning from his vain search, discovers Chloe's sandal—is overcome with emotion, and drops to the ground in a swoon.

While he lies unconscious, the figures of three nymphs materialize in shadowy outline from the rocks, and

151

stepping down from their pedestals, dance about him in slow, mysterious rhythm. (To emphasize the eerie, mist-like quality of this scene, Ravel uses the eoliphone or *windmaschine* of Richard Strauss.) The nymphs bend over the unfortunate lover and invoke their god to his assistance. Daphnis, in his dreams, sees the mighty figure of Pan in the background, and prostrates himself before the vision. Night falls, and the distant choruses sing an appealing refrain.

Gradually the music changes to the vigorous and martial tones of the "Danse guerrière." As the light returns to the stage a pirates' camp is seen in the midst of picturesque rocks at the edge of the sea. The brigands come in, laden with booty, and perform a wild pæan of triumph.

Bryaxis, chief of the pirates, orders Chloe to be brought in, and commands her to dance for their entertainment. With bound hands, she pleads vainly with him; then, finding he is obdurate, she tries to slip away. The pirate chief is furious at this subterfuge; he picks her up roughly and starts to carry her off, when suddenly—to the heavy palpitation of bass violins, which swells into a terrifying crescendo of the entire orchestra and creates in the listeners a panic of terror—a huge shadow appears on the mountainside: the great god Pan has come to Chloe's rescue. While the scene melts into the shadows the pirates flee in panic, and Chloe remains alone, crowned with an aureole of light.

The third and last scene is again at the edge of the

sacred wood of the nymphs. Daphnis lies sleeping; the murmurs of muted strings and flutes produce a miraculous effect of night changing slowly to luminous dawn. Birds with faint twitterings announce the coming day, and finally the radiance of the rising sun illuminates the scene with unearthly splendor. In this evocation of dawn and the invisible voices of Nature, Ravel has written one of his most exquisitely descriptive pieces of music.

As Daphnis awakens, Chloe appears, surrounded by shepherds and shepherdesses, and the combined orchestra and chorus swell to a crescendo of joyous thanksgiving. Daphnis, embracing her ecstatically, realizes that his dream was a reality and that the god Pan has miraculously saved his love. The moving theme that describes the reunion of Daphnis and Chloe is one of the most touching expressions of love that ever escaped Ravel's diffident and reserved nature.

An old shepherd explains that Pan saved Chloe because he once loved the nymph Syrinx. The following exposition is written on Ravel's score:

Daphnis and Chloe mime the story of Pan and Syrinx. Chloe impersonates the young nymph wandering over the meadow. Daphnis as Pan appears and declares his love for her. The nymph repulses him; the god becomes more insistent. She disappears among the reeds. In desperation he plucks some stalks, fashions a flute, and on it plays a melancholy tune. Chloe comes out and imitates by her dance the accents of the flute.

The dance grows more and more animated. In mad whirlings, Chloe falls into the arms of Daphnis. Before the altar of the nymphs he swears on two sheep his fidelity. Young girls enter; they are dressed as Bacchantes and shake their tambourines. Daphnis and Chloe embrace tenderly. A group of young men come on the stage.

Joyous tumult. A general dance. Daphnis and Chloe.

Daphnis and Chloe is acclaimed the finest ballet France has produced, and Ravel's greatest masterpiece. He called it [3] a *"symphonie chorégraphique en trois parties . . . une vaste fresque musicale, moins soucieuse d'archaïsme que de fidélité à la Grèce de mes rêves. . . ."* * Of it Jean Marnold says: [4]

> The score abounds in tableaux of the most exquisite plastic beauty; among these the appearance of the gracious nymphs in the twilit shadow of a dream is a page without precedent or model in the whole of music. . . . Never has the magic of picturesque sonority reached such an intensity.
>
> *Daphnis and Chloe* really constitutes a "musical drama" which offers the coherence and unity of a vast symphony. All of this music holds itself together and lives its own autonomous existence, to such an extent that the preliminary introduction of the leitmotifs would make even a blind man understand and follow the scenic action.

The lyrical beauty of *Daphnis and Chloe* is enriched and strengthened by a depth and power not previously found in Ravel's music—force within restraint. These qualities raised him at once to a new and more important position in the musical world. Although the ballet founded on this work was not entirely successful,

* "A choreographic symphony in three parts . . . a vast musical fresco, less true to archaic tradition than to the Greece of my dreams. . . ."

Daphnis and Chloe has achieved universal renown in symphonic form. Two orchestral suites, containing the best of the music, have been drawn from the score, and these have been heard all over the world.

At the first presentation of the ballet, Ravel as usual arrived late. Just as the curtain went up he appeared in the corridor of the Châtelet Theater, resplendent in full evening dress (was it the midnight-blue outfit?) and carrying a large package under his arm.

"Dépêchez-vous, mon cher, c'est déjà commencé. . . !"

"Yes," Ravel replied, "in just a moment!" He hurried to the Godebskis' loge and there, unwrapping his package, presented Cipa's sister Missia with a large, gorgeously dressed Chinese doll.

XIII

THE "GREAT YEAR OF BALLETS"

RAVEL IN 1912—"VALSES NOBLES ET SENTIMEN-
TALES"—"ADÉLAÏDE OU LE LANGAGE DES FLEURS"—
"MA MÈRE L'OYE" MADE INTO A BALLET—STRAVINSKY
AND SCHOENBERG—ORCHESTRATION OF "KHOVAN-
TCHINA"—"TROIS POÈMES DE STÉPHANE MALLARMÉ"

AFTER Joseph Ravel's death Maurice moved with
his mother to an apartment at 4, avenue Carnot, on the
edge of the Place de l'Etoile facing the Arc de Tri-
omphe. Edouard, his younger brother, still lived with
them, and continued his work at the factory at Levallois-
Perret where automobile and machine parts were manu-
factured. Edouard spent much of his time with his good
friends the Bonnets. Monsieur Bonnet had been Joseph
Ravel's right-hand man at the factory, and remained as
manager after the latter's death. When Mme Ravel
passed away, in 1917, Edouard made his permanent
home with the Bonnets, first in St-Cloud and later at
Levallois-Perret where they eventually built a house next
door to the factory.

Edouard Ravel—of kindly but retiring disposition—

was a hard worker, up and out at an early hour, and seldom at home when his brother was there. Maurice, on the other hand, was a true *noctambule*, who never went to bed until every other possibility had been exhausted. He liked to spend long hours over an *apéritif* at some café (in later years he had a passion for nightclubs) and often, after his friends had retired exhausted, Ravel would start out on one of his interminable walks which were not infrequently prolonged until dawn.

Mme Ravel, now a gentle white-haired woman, still held first place in her son's heart. "No other woman could have lived with Maurice," Mme Bonnet remarked one day; "his habits were too irregular. . . . He got up late and often worked all day in his pajamas. About seven his mother would say: *'Il est sept heures, Maurice, nous allons bientôt souper.'*

" *'Pas possible! . . . Je vais faire un petit tour d'abord.'*

"He would hastily put on a few clothes over his pajamas and start out for a walk.

"At nine, no Ravel. At ten, he still had not come back. Then his mother—only too well accustomed to her son's lack of time sense—would turn to the servant: *'Je n'attendrai pas plus longtemps,'* and have her supper. At eleven or twelve Maurice would finally return, exhausted from his walk, but still unconscious of the hour. He had been 'working his music' the entire time."

Ravel's appearance in 1910 was considerably changed. Instead of the famous beard—trimmed à la

Van Dyke, or square-cut—or the luxurious *favoris*, he now "raised his mask, uncovering at last his true face" (as Roland-Manuel describes the metamorphosis) and from that time remained entirely clean-shaven. His music also changed and began to take on a new, more incisive and clear-cut form. In addition to *Daphnis and Chloe* he began work on a new composition which he called: *Valses nobles et sentimentales*, a "chain of waltzes after the example of Schubert." "*A la virtuosité qui faisait le fond de* Gaspard de la Nuit *succède une écriture nettement plus clarifiée, qui durcit l'harmonie et accuse les reliefs.*" *[1]

Valses nobles et sentimentales was, as Ravel has indicated on his score, dedicated to "the delicious pleasure of useless occupation." It consists of seven short waltzes and a longer epilogue which combines and elaborates the previous themes. The opening waltz is a startling combination of apparent discords; these at first shock the listener, but upon analysis are found to be entirely rational and legitimate. There are no introductory measures—the first waltz plunges at once into harsh chords in constant repetition.

The second waltz is languid and voluptuous; the third lively, with quaint and unusual tone combinations. The five succeeding waltzes continue through an entire gamut of color and feeling. There is amazing variety in their

* "To the virtuosity underlying *Gaspard de la Nuit* is added a much simpler form of writing, which emphasizes the harmony and strengthens its outlines."

Ravel "lifts his mask" and appears clean-shaven.

measures—seduction, drama, and pathos are represented. The epilogue, full of lyrical beauty and ending in soft, sentimental tones, is especially appealing. *"Une sensualité un peu sèche anime cette musique. Frissons électriques, souplesses de chat: délices baudelairiennes."* * [2]

Valses nobles et sentimentales was the most daring composition Ravel had so far produced. He had just completed the score when the Société Musicale Indépendante—now a year old—decided to give an anonymous concert of works of contemporary musicians. The audience was to pass judgment and guess the authors of the various numbers.

On the evening of the concert Ravel sat in a box with some of his friends, waiting to see the reaction of the audience to the *Valses* (played by Louis Aubert and also dedicated to him). By this time Ravel enjoyed an enviable reputation as one of the outstanding younger composers, and a new work from his pen usually received high commendation from discriminating listeners. Those who were gathered at the S.M.I. concert of anonymous works formed a seasoned audience, accustomed to modern music.

But they proved singularly disconcerted by the *Valses nobles et sentimentales.* Some of them were even roused to fury; cat-calls and hisses resounded through the hall —scarcely anyone had a good word to say for the work.

* "A rather dry sensuality animates this music. Electrical thrills, feline flexibility: Baudelairian delights."

Few if any guessed who the composer was (some thought it was Satie), and Ravel had to listen to the most ferocious criticism from friends who had no suspicion that he was actually the one who had written the offending music.

Through the ensuing hullabaloo Ravel made no sign. Later, when the critics discovered who had written the *Valses,* they revised their judgment and found qualities they had failed to discover at the first hearing. This experience proved a lesson to Ravel in the true value of criticism.

Valses nobles et sentimentales was written originally for the piano, but the following spring Ravel orchestrated the work. Mlle Trouhanova, whose *concerts de danse* included interpretations of classical and modern works, asked Ravel if she could use the *Valses* on one of her programs. He was glad to consent, since he was especially interested in the dance and ballet at that time. *Daphnis and Chloe* had recently been completed (though he was still polishing the "Bacchanale"); and he now proceeded to develop a dramatic outline for a stage presentation of the *Valses.* This work was rechristened in its ballet form *Adélaïde, ou le langage des fleurs.*

The scene is laid in the period of 1820, in the salon of a beautiful courtesan who expresses her amorous moods through the medium of flowers. As the curtain rises to the music of the first waltz a number of couples are seen dancing. Vases of flowers decorate the room, and the graceful hostess goes from one to the other, in-

160

haling their fragrance. She pauses longest over the tuberoses (signifying voluptuousness).

Lorédan, an elegant and handsome young man, comes in as the second waltz begins. He offers Adélaïde a ranunculus ("your beauty is full of appeal")—then a hawthorn blossom, which indicates hope. But she is not moved by his entreaties; she chooses a white syringa, emblem of fraternal love, and hands it to the disappointed suitor. He refuses this answer and seizes an iris —"my heart is in flames"—which Adélaïde accepts, and putting it to her lips rewards him with a black iris, confession of deep love. Lorédan, throwing himself at her feet, presents her with a heliotrope—"I love you!" —but her reply is merely a marguerite signifying: "I will consider."

In the third waltz Adélaïde pulls off the petals of the marguerite, one by one, and finds that Lorédan truly loves her. But just as she is about to yield to his embraces the Duke, a wealthy suitor for her favors, arrives with a bouquet of sunflowers—promise of riches—and a necklace of diamonds. She is overcome by the Duke's generosity and gives him a flower from her corsage.

As Adélaïde dances with the Duke, Lorédan (in the sixth waltz) pursues his fickle lady. But she has eyes only for her wealthy suitor, and the rejected lover withdraws into an alcove from where he watches the gay company with melancholy resignation.

In the last scene, or epilogue, the guests retire; but the Duke lingers, hoping Adélaïde will invite him to

remain. She, however, holds out to him a branch of
acacia—emblem of platonic love; he understands the
language of flowers, and with a sad bow departs. Now
Lorédan advances hopefully, but the capricious Adélaïde presents him with a poppy—forgetfulness. He
thrusts it aside and rushes from the room.

Adélaïde, left alone, opens the window of her balcony
and stands there with a tuberose in her hand while the
music recalls the theme of the first waltz. Suddenly
Lorédan appears at a neighboring balcony. He holds a
twig of cypress and a marigold, symbols of despair,
and pulling out a pistol raises it to his head. Adélaïde
repents her fickleness, throws Lorédan a red rose, and
the curtain descends as the two lovers fall into each
other's arms.

Ravel orchestrated *Adélaïde, ou le langage des fleurs*
in two weeks' time, and himself directed Mlle Trouhanova's ballet at the Châtelet Theater on April 22.
(This was only the second time that he had directed an
orchestra—the *Overture to Shéhérazade* in 1899 was the
first.) There were several other numbers on Mlle Trouhanova's program, but none had so great a triumph as
Adélaïde. Its first presentation at the S.M.I. had been
a notable failure; in its ballet form it was an even more
notable success.

The fascination of seeing music come to life through
the dramatic medium of the colorful ballet gave Ravel
at this time an especial interest in the stage. The year

1912 was his *grande année de ballets*. In addition to *Daphnis and Chloe* and *Adélaïde* he decided to orchestrate and turn into a ballet the little piano suite *Ma Mère l'Oye* which he had composed years before for Jean and Mimie Godebski.

The charming fairy-tales adapted themselves delightfully to ballet form. Ravel wisely decided to keep to the childlike simplicity of the original; he used a small orchestra of thirty-two pieces and kept the details down to an almost lilliputian scale—at least, that was the effect of the original presentation at the small Théatre des Arts on the boulevard des Batignolles.

Ravel conceived the idea of presenting a scene within a scene, to emphasize the miniature effect. Two little turbaned *négrillons* pulled the curtains of the inner stage and changed the scenes—charmingly designed by Drésa —before the eyes of the audience.

In the ballet version of *Ma Mère l'Oye*, Ravel uses the story of the Sleeping Beauty as the main theme, but with substantial variations from the earlier form.* First the Princess Florine is seen dancing about her beautiful garden, while her old nurse sits at the spinning-wheel. The princess falls against the spindle and pricks herself; there is great excitement as courtiers and ladies-in-waiting gather about the fainting princess. They dance a solemn *pavane* as she is laid out on her couch. A fairy appears to watch over the princess and to bring dreams to her enchanted slumbers.

* See Chapter XI.

The following scenes show the dreams of the be-witched Princess Florine. First Beauty and the Beast begin their conversations, which end with the magical transformation of the Beast into a handsome prince. The two little Negroes change the scene of the inner stage, holding up a banner with the name of the next dream.

After Beauty and the Beast comes Petit Poucet who, with his brothers, advances sorrowfully through the for-est, dropping crumbs of bread which he hopes will show the way home. But while the children sleep, the birds eat all the crumbs. . . .

Next is told the story of Laideronnette, empress of the pagodas, and her lover Serpentin Vert—a whirl of oriental dances and colorful costumes. As this dream ends the two little Negroes fade away, and the Princess Florine is left alone in her garden. Prince Charming arrives and discovers the sleeping princess. With a kiss he awakens her to life, and the ballet comes to a close with the music of the Jardin Féerique.

Ma Mère l'Oye, Adélaïde ou le langage des fleurs, and *Daphnis and Chloe* all saw their first presentation in less than six months. In truth, 1912 was Ravel's "great year of ballets."

By 1913 Diaghileff's ballets had become celebrated for their novelty. In a search for unusual material, he thought of combining the powers of two of his most original and effective orchestrators. Stravinsky and

Ravel had both provided him with superlative material; he suggested that they make a new score for a work of Moussorgsky.

When this Russian composer died at the untimely age of forty-two he left a number of unfinished compositions, including an opera called *Khovantchina*. Rimsky-Korsakoff had completed this after Moussorgsky's death, but Diaghileff felt that a new orchestration would be more effective, and asked Stravinsky and Ravel to collaborate in producing it.

Stravinsky was living at that time in Switzerland, at Clarens on the edge of Lake Geneva, and Ravel decided to join him there so that they could work on *Khovantchina* together. Ravel usually spent his summers on the Basque coast, at Ciboure, St-Jean-de-Luz, or Biarritz, with his mother. Aside from one or two trips to Switzerland and a journey to Holland in 1905, he had until that time done very little traveling.

Igor Stravinsky was seven years younger than Ravel. His dynamic Slav temperament was in direct contrast to that of the polished and self-controlled French composer; yet the two understood each other perfectly. Stravinsky's bold harmonizations, his rebellion at old forms and creation of new values fitted into the pattern of Ravel's own musical conceptions. Both composers delighted in setting legend and fantasy to music, and they admired the same poets. (In 1910 Stravinsky wrote a song to Verlaine's poem "Un grand sommeil noir"—the

165

same poem that had provided the text for one of Ravel's earliest songs.)

Stravinsky in his earlier days was greatly interested in, and to a certain extent influenced by, the works of the German composer Arnold Schoenberg. The latter was born in Vienna in 1874, a year before Ravel, and is perhaps the most original figure in the world of music today. Although Schoenberg's foundation is classical, he has developed away from tonality and melodic progression to a region of intricate structure without parallel in musical annals. Ravel considered Schoenberg an extraordinarily gifted musician, but his own essentially French spirit, with its love of clarity and ordered form, made it difficult for him to understand the elaborate workings of the German composer's mind. He felt that Schoenberg's expression was unnecessarily complicated and that his line of musical reasoning could not go beyond certain limits. A "school of discord," he called it. It was Ravel's belief that the music of the future would return to melody rather than experiment further with atonality.

Schoenberg's *Pierrot Lunaire* and Stravinsky's music nevertheless had a direct influence on a group of songs which Ravel began during his stay in Switzerland in the summer of 1913: "Trois poèmes de Stéphane Mallarmé," with accompaniment of piano, string quartet, two flutes and two clarinets. One of Ravel's earliest songs —"Sainte"—was written to a poem of Mallarmé; now he chose three others: "Soupir," "Placet futile," and "Surgi de la croupe et du bond"—the first dedicated to Stravinsky, the second to Florent Schmitt, and the third to Erik Satie. "Soupir" is a long sigh of melancholy, with soft, monotonous accompaniment. "Placet futile" glitters with arpeggios and rich harmonies. "Surgi de la croupe et du bond" was added the following summer during Ravel's visit to St-Jean-de-Luz.

In these songs Ravel has continued and extended to extreme limits the direction he took in *Valses nobles et sentimentales*. He reaches "a rarefied atmosphere with the brilliance, transparency and hardness of the diamond, the frigidity of ice. . . ." Yet, though Ravel was constantly experimenting with new forms, he cannot justly be called a revolutionary. Tristan Klingsor says: [3]

It is almost unbelievable that the academicians did not understand how classical he really was—classical in his desire for order in all things, in the placing of his periods, in the melodic design, in harmony, in instrumentation. When he innovated, and certainly as harmonist he did this frequently, it was in drawing unexpected but logical consequences from old principles. . . . He showed the way to others. . . . In reality all that he did was to go farther along the path which his predecessors had blazed.

Three numbers for piano complete the list of Ravel's compositions during 1913. *Prélude* was published by Durand, as were all of his later works with the exception of *A la Manière de* (a) *Borodine* (b) *Chabrier.**

* Published by Mathot.

These, also written in 1913, were tributes to two musicians whom Ravel had admired since his early youth.

In 1917 Diaghileff suggested another ballet to Ravel, using the libretto of the Italian poet Cangiullo. Ravel confirmed by letter his intention of writing this ballet, but the work was never undertaken—or, at least, no trace of it has been found. The following year Diaghileff presented a ballet in Spain called *Jardins d'Aranjuez*, using themes from Chabrier and Fauré and from Ravel's *Rapsodie espagnole*.

He later commissioned Ravel to write an "apotheosis of the waltz"; but when the score of *La Valse* was brought to him he decided that it was unsuited to his purpose. Ravel was deeply offended. He interpreted Diaghileff's refusal of his manuscript as a personal reflection on his ability as an artist. There followed a serious break between the two men which was never healed.

In 1925 Diaghileff and Ravel met again in Monte Carlo. Diaghileff, who wished to forget the past, held out his hand, but Ravel turned away and would not agree to a reconciliation. Diaghileff, accustomed to flattery and adulation from all those who surrounded him, was furious—and not without cause—at this rebuff. He challenged Ravel to a duel, but friends were fortunately able to prevent the encounter.

Nearly all of Ravel's orchestrated works have been produced in ballet form at one time or another. His

Edouard Ravel, only brother of Maurice

(*upper*) The piano in Ravel's study at Le Belvédère

(*lower*) The gold and white bedroom at Le Belvédère,
decorated by Ravel

deep sense of rhythm makes his music singularly well fitted to interpretation through the dance. On the other hand those of his compositions which were written primarily for the ballet have achieved their greatest triumphs on symphonic programs. This is proof of the extraordinary craftsmanship and musical appeal of his works.

XIV

RAVEL FIGHTS FOR FRANCE

ON THE BASQUE COAST——TRIO FOR PIANO,
VIOLIN, AND CELLO——RAVEL IN THE WORLD
WAR——HIS LETTERS FROM THE FRONT——DEATH
OF MME RAVEL——"LE TOMBEAU DE COUPERIN"

EARLY in the summer of 1914 Ravel traveled to the
Basque coast and established himself at St-Jean-de-Luz,
just south of Biarritz. The vast expanse of ocean and—
facing it—the panorama of the Pyrenees never failed to
bring him inspiration and refreshment. These were more
than native surroundings: the enduring qualities of
mountains, sea, and rocky coast were symbols of the
loyalty of his own nature—a loyalty which attached him
with deep devotion to his family and friends, and bound
him to the scenes of his early childhood.

One or more of the Apaches could usually be found
in the neighborhood during the summer months, and it
was not unusual to hear the Borodin theme whistled in
the streets of Ciboure or St-Jean-de-Luz. Soon after, perhaps, a small figure would be seen emerging in picturesque bathing costume: brilliant peignoir and scarlet
cap. Ravel was an excellent swimmer; this and walking

were his only sports. He and his friends took long excursions down the coast, across the French border into Spain, or into the mountains.

A number of concerts were usually organized during the summer. The municipalities of Ciboure, St-Jean-de-Luz, and Biarritz boasted an excellent chorus, and it may be that Ravel's songs for mixed chorus, composed in 1916 while he was on the Basque coast, were written for this organization. There are three songs in the group: "Nicolette," "Trois beaux oiseaux du Paradis," and "Ronde," to be sung without accompaniment. Ravel himself wrote the words.

Years later—in 1930—the little town of Ciboure decided to honor its illustrious native son by renaming the Quai de la Nivelle "Quai Maurice Ravel" and by placing a plaque on the house where he was born. An important festival was planned for the occasion; in the afternoon a brilliant exhibition match of the celebrated Basque pelota took place, and in the evening there was a concert of Ravel's works in Biarritz. Several of France's most outstanding musicians traveled south to take part in this affair. Robert Casadesus played *Jeux d'eau*, and Jacques Thibaud, with the composer at the piano, performed the violin sonata. Several others, including the singer Madeleine Grey, contributed their talents to this program.

Ravel met Madeleine Grey early in 1914 when she made her debut with the Pasdeloup Orchestra. At that time he came back stage and congratulated the young singer ("*à sa façon, c'est à dire à la fois très discrète-ment et très chaleureusement . . .*"[1]) and asked her if she would like to try some of his songs. A few days later he sent her his Hebraic melodies "Kaddisch" and "L'Enigme éternelle" which he had recently completed. In the years following he frequently chose her as inter-preter of his songs.

Ravel had always wished to write a composition using the Basque themes of his native land. He spent some time on a work to be called "Zaspiak-Bat," but forsook this in 1914 for a new project in chamber music—a trio for piano, cello, and violin.

In this composition Ravel admitted that he was in-spired by the early trios of Saint-Saëns—in at least the form of the work. Ravel's Trio, however, is much simpler in melodic outline; it is remarkable for the clearness of its style and for the depth which it achieves through stark simplicity. He here dispenses with every-thing which is not absolutely essential; in general form the Trio continues in the direction taken first by *Valses nobles et sentimentales*. Roland-Manuel says that it pos-sesses a "magisterial character" far removed from the melancholy ardor of the String Quartet. He adds that Ravel often said he would willingly have exchanged the *savoir* of his trio for the *pouvoir* of his more youthful Quartet.

In August, 1914, while Ravel was working on his Trio at St-Jean-de-Luz, the storm which had been hover-ing menacingly across the European horizon burst into sudden fury. France found herself plunged into war, and Ravel, who in his quiet way was an ardent patriot, sought immediately to enlist in spite of the violent protests of his friends and family. They tried to show him that his value as a composer was more important to his country than any personal sacrifice he could make in actual warfare. They knew too that he had not the physical strength to endure the hardships of life at the front. Although he had never suffered any serious illness, he was not robust nor accustomed to any sort of rigorous existence.

The authorities recognized these limitations and refused to accept Ravel as a soldier. He was bitterly disappointed, and in an effort to serve in some capacity volunteered to care for the wounded soldiers who began to arrive in great numbers at the hospitals in Biarritz. In October he wrote to Roland-Manuel: [2]

Je le sais bien, mon cher ami, que je travaille pour la patrie en faisant de la musique! Du moins, on me l'a assez dit pour m'en convaincre depuis deux mois; d'abord pour m'empêcher de me présenter, ensuite pour me consoler de mon échec. On n'a rien empêché, et je ne me console pas. . . .

Je veille aussi les blessés toutes les semaines, ce qui est assez absorbant: c'est inouï le nombre, sinon la variété de besoins que peuvent avoir quarante bons-hommes dans le courant d'une nuit!

Je fais également de la musique: impossible de continuer Zaspiak-Bat, *dont les documents sont restés à Paris. Délicat de travailler la* Cloche engloutie. . . . *Je commence deux séries de morceaux de piano: 1—une suite française—non, ce n'est pas ce que vous croyez: la Marseillaise n'y figurera point, et*

il y aura une forlane, une gigue; pas de tango, cependant. 2—
une Nuit romantique avec spleen, chasse infernale, nonne
*maudite, etc.**

Ravel returned to Paris still rebellious because he had
been refused for military service. "I do not yet risk
receiving the Croix de Guerre," he wrote, "although I
live in the midst of the horrible dangers of a rear-line
camp (*accidents de métro, combats à la manille, minis-*
terès qui sautent, etc.)." [3] He finally decided that his
slender frame and light weight might make him accept-
able for aviation service; but this too having been refused, he enlisted in the motor-convoy department and
was at last accepted as driver of a *camion* (motor-
truck). He left for the front in March 1916.

The war proved a devastating experience to Ravel,
morally as well as physically. At first, however, like

---

* I am quite aware, my dear friend, that I am working for my
country when I compose! At least, I have been told this often
enough for the past two months to convince me; first to prevent
me from enlisting, afterward to console me for my disappointment. I wasn't prevented, and I am not consoled . . .

I likewise care for the wounded every week, which is absorbing
enough: the unheard-of number, as well as variety, of needs which
forty men can have in the course of one night!

I am also composing; impossible to continue *Zaspiak-Bat*, the
sketches for which were left in Paris. It is a delicate matter. to
work on the *Sunken Bell* [because of the war] . . . I am beginning two series of piano pieces: first, a French suite—no, this is
not what you think: there will be no Marseillaise, and it will have
a forlane, gigue; but no tango. Second, a Romantic Night with
spleen, infernal hunt, accursed nun, etc.

(The *Suite française* became the *Tombeau de Couperin*, but the
Nuit romantique never materialized.)

many another he was more fascinated than shocked by the terrible things he saw. He was surprised at his own reactions: [4]

Et pourtant je suis pacifique; je n'ai jamais été courageux. Mais voilà: j'ai eu la curiosité de l'aventure. Elle a une telle saveur qu'elle devient nécessaire. Que ferai-je, que feront beaucoup d'autres aprè la guerre? *

Gradually, however, the horror of his daily life began to penetrate the armor he had built over his sensitive nature, and he became increasingly indignant at the stupidity and uselessness of the war. [5]

Oh le pessimisme stupide de ces imbéciles . . . cet égoïsme borné, ces opinions de taupes . . . de petits cris me dérangent: c'est une pauvre souris qui s'est prise au piège de rat.†

One day as Ravel was driving his camion (which he had named "Rosalie") near Verdun, in the midst of the deafening thunder of cannons and all the horrible tumult of battle the guns were suddenly silenced, and a moment of supernatural quiet succeeded the dreadful uproar. Dawn was just breaking, and the world seemed to have awakened from a ghastly nightmare. All at once a bird began to sing. . . .

It seemed like a miracle to the war-weary musician.

---

* And yet I am peace-loving; I have never been brave. But there it is: I am curious for adventure. It has such a fascination that it becomes a necessity. What shall I do, what will many others do, after the war?

† Oh, the stupid pessimism of these imbeciles . . . this near-sighted self-centeredness, these mole-like opinions . . . small cries disturb me: it is a poor mouse caught in a rat-trap.

He loved the songs of birds, and could imitate all those he heard. The notes of the little warbler, lifting its voice almost in the midst of the battle's inferno, seemed like a message from above—an assurance that life was good and that a higher power still ruled the world. The incident made such an impression on Ravel that he determined to write a melody: *"La fauvette indifférente."* [6] But by the time the war was ended he was too disillusioned to develop this simple theme of faith triumphant over chaos.

While Ravel was at the front a "National League for the Defense of French Music" was inaugurated by a group of ardent if narrow-minded patriots. They felt that the works of German composers should no longer be included in concerts given in France, and wanted Ravel to give the project his personal approval.

Ravel's reply—a long letter written from the front— is a document of clear and impartial reasoning, and a merited rebuke not only to his own countrymen but to those who even in the United States confused artistic with national issues during the hysteria of the war years: [7]

I regret that I am not able to concur in your ideas. . . . I cannot follow you when you state the principle that "the role of music is both economic and social." I have never considered that "for the safety of our artistic national patrimony" it is necessary "to forbid the public performance in France of contemporary German and Austrian compositions." . . .
It would be even dangerous for French composers to ignore systematically the works of their foreign fellow-artists, and

thus to form a sort of national coterie; our musical art, so rich at present, would soon degenerate if it shut itself within such bigoted formulas. . . .

It matters little to me that Mr. Schoenberg, for instance, is of Austrian nationality. He is none the less a musician of high merit, and his interesting experiments have had a happy influence on certain allied composers, and even with us. Still more am I delighted that MM. Bartok, Kodaly, and their disciples are Hungarian and manifest it in their works with so much zest. . . .

Ravel's letter aroused a storm of resentment in the "Ligue Nationale pour la Défense de la Musique Française." A sarcastic reply from the president included the following threat: [8]

. . . I am delighted to learn to what degree you appreciate the "high merit" of the musician Schoenberg, the "zest" of MM. Bartok, Kodaly, and their disciples. The National League will be here at the opportune moment to advise the public of your admiration in the case of an eventual sacrifice, most unfortunate, of your own music. . . .

Ravel sincerely believed that music could not be restricted by national boundaries; he knew it to be a universal language which appeals to the heart of all mankind. His wartime championship of the enemy's music brought him to a broader understanding of much that he had criticized in his younger days, and especially of Wagner's works. In the years following he came to appreciate and even admire the great German whom he had once called *"le grand cauchemar harmonique."*

177

Ravel tried once again in May of 1916 to enter the aviation service. But when he was examined it was discovered not only that he was physically unfit for the aviation service, but also that the two months he had already passed at the front had seriously affected his general health. Ravel, thinking in terms of his motor-truck, wrote: [9]

Il n'y a pas que le carburateur qui soit atteint. Le moteur lui-même ne marche que sur trois pattes. . . . Il n'est pas jusqu'à la boîte de vitesse qui ne laisse à désirer. Pourvu que la direction n'aille pas se fausser maintenant. . . .*

His condition alarmed him less than the possibility that his mother might hear of it. Mme Ravel had been failing seriously since her son's departure for the front. He was deeply concerned about the one he loved best in all the world.[10]

Je ne souffre vraiment que d'une chose, c'est de ne pouvoir embrasser ma pauvre Maman. . . . Oui . . . cependant il y a autre chose: la musique. Je croyais l'avoir oubliée. Depuis quelques jours elle revient, tyrannique. Je ne pense plus qu'à ça. Je suis sûr que j'aurais été en pleine période de production. . . .†

* It isn't only the carburetor that is affected. The motor itself is hobbling about on three legs. . . . Even the gear-shift leaves much to be desired. Here's hoping that the steering-gear will not likewise go wrong. . . .

† I really suffer from one thing only, and that is not to be able to embrace my poor mother. . . . Yes . . . there is something else: Music. I thought I had forgotten it. These last few days it has returned, like a tyrant. I can think of nothing else. I am sure I should have been in the midst of a period of full production. . . .

He had all but forgotten music in the horrors of war, and even feared that his creative ability had been destroyed. But now the compelling voice of his mistress returned, and he was tormented by an urge to compose.[11]

*Je n'ai jamais été aussi musicien: je déborde d'inspiration, de projets de toutes sortes, musique de chambre, symphonies, ballets. . . .**

Ravel wished to honor the memory of certain of his close friends who had fallen during the tragic years of the war. He decided to compose a suite of various numbers, each dedicated individually to one of these comrades—the entire work to be a tribute (*hommage*) to the great Couperin. Of all the early French composers Couperin appealed most to Ravel, as Rameau did to Debussy. It has already been remarked that Debussy wrote *Hommage à Rameau;* Ravel now planned *Le Tombeau de Couperin*—a development of the "Suite française" he had projected two years before in St-Jean-de-Luz.

It was impossible, however, to write music at the front. Ravel, fretting at the hardships and the restrictions which kept him from his work, fell really ill. He spent several weeks in a hospital near the front, and then returned to Paris to convalesce. But there a new blow awaited him: his beloved mother passed away early in January of 1917.

* I have never been so full of music: I overflow with inspiration, with all sorts of projects, chamber music, symphonies, ballets. . . .

Ravel was stupefied by this tragedy. He had somehow never realized that one day he must lose his mother. She was so completely a part of his life that he could not imagine existence without her. His friends were unable to console him—he wandered about the streets of Paris like a lost soul, and finally, believing his health sufficiently improved and anxious to forget his sorrow in action, he returned to Châlons-sur-Marne near the front.

There followed a period of intense depression, both physical and moral, and it became evident that he could no longer be of use to his country in active work. He was released from service, and the summer of 1917 found him in Normandy, determined to complete the *Tombeau de Couperin*. *"Enfin, je travaille. Ça fait supporter tant de choses. . . ."* [12]

Ravel asked a friend to send him several of Liszt's works, including *Mazeppa* and the *Etudes*. He never tired of analyzing and studying Liszt's scores; yet if *Mazeppa* and the *Etudes* served as models for *Le Tombeau de Couperin*, certainly this influence is not to be detected in the finished composition. Nothing could be farther removed from Liszt's elaborate, somewhat flamboyant style than the classic purity of Ravel's tribute to his fallen comrades. *Le Tombeau de Couperin* represents the extreme limit of Ravel's effort to express himself in the simplest possible manner; a transparent serenity full of color and feeling pervades these pages . . . *"un adieu dans un sourire."*

These pieces, consecrated under the invocation of Couperin-le-grand to the memory of friends lost during the war, have, in their calm full of grace, more charm than melancholy. It is as if Ravel wished to protest that flowers are not sad of themselves, but only through the circumstance of their offering, which has nothing to do with the passer-by.[13]

The "Tombeau" form dates from the seventeenth century, and is a musical "homage" dedicated to a deceased person. Yet in spite of its tragic associations Ravel's *Tombeau de Couperin* is neither somber nor sad. The six numbers of the piano suite are written in dance form: *Prelude, Fugue, Forlane, Rigaudon, Menuet, Toccata.* (The last of these was inscribed to the memory of Captain de Morliave, Marguerite Long's husband; she later became the first interpreter of Ravel's piano concerto in G.)

Prelude is a sprightly dance with an eerie quality which, in places, recalls the music of bagpipes. It rises and falls again and again, ending with a trill which is discordant but so delicately balanced that it charms rather than disturbs the listener.

Fugue presents its theme first in the upper, then in the lower, register—a murmuring dialogue of music. *Forlane* is in more serious mood, with a rhythmic refrain of austere nobility. The forlane was originally an Italian dance of the early eighteenth century, in 6–4 or 6–8 time, somewhat similar to the gigue in character.

Rigaudon is another old dance form which originated in the French Provence, and was there rendered in a lively, jumping manner. Ravel's *Rigaudon* has great dynamic rhythm. Strong chords alternate in loud and soft tones, and then change to a plaintive melody carried by the wood winds with pizzicato string accompaniment. At the end there is an abrupt return to the beginning refrain.

Menuet is perhaps the most charming of the suite. It has a classical theme of haunting simplicity and melancholy charm. The middle part—a pure and moving refrain—is sung by the violins; and finally the original melody, with new and startling harmonizations, brings the composition to a close.

Toccata, last of the group (not included in the orchestral suite), is a brilliant and forceful number which in some ways recalls *Scarbo* of the *Gaspard de la Nuit* suite.

Le Tombeau de Couperin was to have been presented in the spring of 1918; but the bombardment of Paris, which threw everyone into a panic, put a temporary stop to all artistic activities. April 1919 saw the first performance of this piano suite at the Salle Gaveau in the rue la Boëtie. It was an enormous success, and the audience cried again and again to have the numbers repeated: *"Forlane!" "Bis—bis!" "Toccata!" "Menuet!"*

One critic, however, still had reservations: Pierre Lalo, writer of so many caustic reviews of Ravel's music, criticized the *Tombeau de Couperin* in a sarcastic article. Commenting on this article Roland-Manuel says: [14]

182

M. Pierre Lalo seldom jokes; doubtless it takes nothing short of a mausoleum to put him in the right spirit. After having praised the charm and precision of the orchestration of "this *Tombeau de Couperin,* where echoes of Chabrier can occasionally be heard, but a small and niggling Chabrier, and also of Fauré, but a Fauré without his poetry"; after complaining that he found in the work none of Couperin's delicacy and sensitiveness, the critic of *Le Temps* (November 16, 1920) borrowed a famous shaft from Rossini, saying: *"Le Tombeau de Couperin par Monsieur Ravel, c'est gentil. Mais combien plus gentil serait un Tombeau de Monsieur Ravel par Couperin!"* *

Two years later Ravel orchestrated four of the numbers: *Prelude, Forlane, Rigaudon,* and *Menuet.* These have also appeared as a ballet (first performance by the Swedish Ballet at the Théâtre des Champs Elysées in Paris). Ravel felt a special affection for *Le Tombeau de Couperin*—perhaps because of its association with his fallen friends. At his death the score of the *Menuet* was found on his piano—the only music visible in his entire establishment.

The simple austerity of *Le Tombeau de Couperin* contains a depth and a poignant sense of humanity not always to be found in Ravel's other compositions. It is pregnant with the suffering through which he was living at the time—his own personal bereavement in the loss of his mother and of his friends fallen at the front, and the tragedy of his country staggering under the burden of war. *Le Tombeau de Couperin* epitomizes all these

* *"Couperin's Tomb* by M. Ravel, that's nice. But how much nicer *Ravel's Tomb* by Couperin would be!"

things in a manner typical of the composer. On the surface no shadow is apparent—all is color, light, and
even gaiety. But beneath this are undertones of tragedy
—the suffering of a spirit that fears lest the world shall
discover what it has to endure.

XV

"THE CHILD AND THE SORCERIES"

RAVEL'S DEPRESSION AFTER THE WAR—THE CHANGE
IN HIS MUSIC—"LA VALSE"—HIS TRAVELS IN EUROPE
AND ENGLAND—THE SONATA FOR VIOLIN AND
CELLO—TZIGANE—"L'ENFANT ET LES SORTILÈGES"

"*JE suis affreusement triste*," wrote Ravel in the late months of 1919. For two years now he had been unable to compose; he feared for a time that he was contracting tuberculosis, and despaired of ever being able to work again. His insomnia, which began during the war, increased to alarming proportions; this affliction never left him, and although he seldom spoke of his sleepless nights, those who were close to him knew how he dreaded the long, dark hours. He was always an inveterate smoker, and now this habit took possession of him with tyrannic force. One cigarette was lighted from another. "*J'aime mieux me passer de manger que de tabac*," he often said.

The war had left an indelible mark on Ravel. Physically he appeared even smaller than before, as if his slight frame had shrunk to still more diminutive dimen-

185

sions. His luxuriant black hair began to turn gray (in a few years he would be completely white) and there was an impression of grayness in his whole character. A profound melancholy possessed him; his smile—a shadow of his former mischievous laughter—became full of tragedy and a certain cynicism. There was bitterness in his heart and a great loneliness; the one he loved most—his mother—had been taken from him, and no other woman ever shared his life.

Ravel's music, too, showed the effects of this great change in character. His revolt against a world where so much suffering could be allowed, his own feeling of frustration and unsatisfactory adjustment to normal life, all these became evident in his music. There is a harshness in his later works which almost completely veils the tenderness of his real nature, and only rarely allows this sensitivity to be seen.

Ravel finally decided that if he could get away from Paris to a quiet spot in the country he might be able to work again. Some friends offered him a haven in the little village of Lapras, and he moved there in December of 1919. A few weeks later the Paris newspapers published a list of those who were to receive the Legion of Honor, and to the surprise of Ravel's friends (who knew his antipathy to decorations) his name was included. As soon as he heard of this he telegraphed at once to Roland-Manuel:[1] *"Merci vivement prière démentir refuse,"* and followed this with a letter saying: "Thanks to all. I have passed my day receiving telegrams. . . .

186

What a ridiculous story! Who could have played such a joke on me?" In spite of the entreaties of his friends (this was the third time the French Government had offered him the decoration), Ravel again refused to accept the honor. When in later years he was reproached for his attitude he would reply with a smile: *"C'était seulement de l'orgeuil de ma part. . . ."* *

Dance rhythms and more particularly the waltz fascinated Maurice Ravel more than any other musical expression. Schubert's waltzes had inspired his *Valses nobles et sentimentales,* and the works of Johann Strauss, with their gay and reckless abandon, suggested to him the brilliant court life of Vienna during the middle nineteenth century. Ravel now decided to write a ballet dedicated to the Viennese waltz.

What changes and suffering had been the fate of Vienna since the war! The gay waltz of her earlier years was now become a mad whirl—an effort to escape from the stark disillusionment of reality. Ravel saw his new ballet as an apotheosis of the waltz, in which all of Vienna's life would be reviewed, from the light-hearted early years to the bleak tragedy of the present.

At the top of the score stands the following description:

Mouvement de Valse Viennoise. Drifting clouds give glimpses, through rifts, of couples waltzing. The clouds gradually scatter, and an immense hall can be seen, filled with a whirling crowd. The scene gradually becomes illumi-

* "That was pure vanity on my part. . . ."

nated. The light of chandeliers bursts forth. An imperial Court about 1855.

La Valse begins with a vague chaotic rumbling—"drifting clouds"—through which the waltz rhythm slowly emerges, accompanied by an ominous undercurrent from the basses. Gradually this rhythm increases and becomes the orthodox waltz of pre-war Vienna, in best Johann Strauss tradition.

Then suddenly there is an abrupt change to harsh, strident chords—a foreboding of the maelstrom to come. The tempo and volume of sound grow stronger; there is a recurrence of the earlier themes, but these are almost submerged in dissonant harmonizations. The waltz continues on and on, now in modern interpretation; the mad whirl increases, and with it comes a feeling of brutal anguish and inexorable fate. The dancers appear to be caught in a vortex. . . . "We must dance, even if we die. . . ." The rhythmic discord seems unending and becomes almost unbearable in its intensity. At last, with a mighty crash of frenzied chords the music ends, and release comes to those who have been caught in the spell of the music. Like *Bolero*, *La Valse* is "a study in crescendo."

La Valse is not only a "danse macabre"—picture of an epoch in which old values and dearly held ideals come crashing to earth in chaos; it portrays the torment of Ravel's own soul at this period. He wrote it during the dreary winter months when he lived alone in the

village of Lapras, away from all friends and cheer; into
La Valse went all the anguish of those bitter days.

Ravel knew that this was one of the finest works he
had written, and was therefore highly indignant—as has
been said—when Diaghileff did not appreciate it nor
see its dramatic possibilities for a ballet. Mme Rubinstein and others have since interpreted *La Valse* in ballet
form, but it remains best known as an orchestral tone-
poem. Soon after its completion it was presented by
Lamoureux and was overwhelmingly successful; with
Bolero it has become Ravel's best-known work.

The outstanding triumph of *La Valse* brought Ravel
into great prominence before the public of the years
after the war. Invitations to conduct were showered on
him from every quarter; he who had always lived a
quiet and retired life found himself traveling from one
European capital to another.

In the fall of 1920 Ravel was invited to conduct and
perform a concert of his own works in Vienna. Austria
was in the midst of inflation, and French currency was
much in demand. One day he went into a leather shop
and chose a portfolio which he ordered sent to his hotel.
The saleswoman upon hearing his name asked if he were
the composer of the famous *Jeux d'eau*. When he said
he was, she begged him to accept the portfolio "as a
sign of her gratitude for such a perfect work." Ravel
never forgot this incident and often spoke of it; that his
music should be so well known in a foreign country was
hard for him to understand.[2]

During the next two years Ravel was chiefly occupied with tours in various countries—Holland, Italy, Spain, and England, Poland, Belgium, Hungary, Rumania, and Switzerland—where he conducted and played his own works. Madeleine Grey accompanied him on his trip through Spain, and has written some interesting souvenirs of this journey in the special number of the *Revue Musicale* called "Hommage à Ravel."

As a traveling companion, she writes, Ravel was entertaining and "constantly creating unexpected situations." He invariably arrived at the station just as the train was about to pull out. *"Une course folle s'ensuivait. . . ."* Ravel (*petit homme élégant*), unable to find a porter, "would accomplish miracles with the best possible good humor. . . . What passer-by would have suspected that this affable man, with his gallant obliviousness of time [*galanterie anachronique*], who stubbornly insisted on carrying my bags without allowing anyone else to touch them, and who caused many smiles because of the disproportion between the objects he carried and his size, was one of the greatest musicians of our time, if not the greatest?" [3]

During the tour through Spain Ravel was entertained by Manuel de Falla in Granada and was enthusiastically acclaimed wherever he went—except, that is, for Malaga. Here the audience gradually—though "discreetly and politely"—deserted the hall in which Ravel and Mlle Grey were giving their concert. At the end of the performance, when the artists came out to bow, they saw only empty seats before them. But Ravel was not disturbed; on the contrary, he thought the incident highly amusing (*"pour lui, l'aventure était follement plaisante"*). He said it made him think of Haydn's *Farewell* Symphony and he thoroughly sympathized with an audience which, though it possessed little understanding and less patience, at least had the courage of its convictions.[4]

The success of Ravel's concerts in the various countries he visited was undoubtedly due more to the appeal of his music than to his ability as a performer. He was a fair but not a brilliant pianist, and in orchestral conducting his interpretations were precise rather than inspired. In England the critics praised his directing, and he was as pleased as a child at their reviews: "According to the papers I am a great, or at least a good, orchestra conductor. I did not expect so much. . . ."[5]

Ravel returned to England on several different tours. In 1926 he was accompanied by the distinguished French cellist, Gerard Hekking. Hekking was particularly impressed by his companion's passion for nocturnal excursions. After a concert the two musicians would return to their hotel to change, and Ravel invariably asked: *"Voulez-vous faire un petit tour?"* They would start out through the dark, unfamiliar streets and walk for hours—sometimes until four in the morning— Ravel keeping up a constant flow of conversation, and never for an instant without a cigarette. He was especially fascinated by the life of the docks at the seaports they visited. Everything interested him—he had an in-satiable, childlike curiosity—this little, indefatigable man who seemed made of steel. His sense of direction was extraordinary; even in completely unfamiliar sur-roundings he always managed to find his way back to the hotel—like a homing pigeon he went straight back to his starting point.

Charlie Chaplin's *Gold Rush* was playing in London while Ravel and Hekking were there, and Ravel went several times to see the picture. "Charlot" had an irre-sistible charm for the French composer. There was some inner bond of understanding between the comedian who could express so much with so little outward show of feeling and the Basque musician with his own reserved but secretly emotional nature. "Charlot may be a cinema actor," said Ravel, "but he goes much farther. He ana-lyses his characters, he is gay—a comedian, yes, but at the same time he has extraordinary depths of sadness and underlying drama."

Ravel disliked the personal publicity that his concerts brought and always tried to elude the enthusiastic hero-worshippers who besieged him wherever he appeared. *"J'ai horreur du publique,"* he confessed. Music to him was an impersonal thing, and not meant for the exploita-tion of the individual. This fundamental of his character is well described in an article by G. Jean-Aubry, an old friend of Ravel's: [6]

His [Ravel's] sole concern was the creation of musical works of art, disassociated from literature and politics. . . .

He was first and foremost a musician, and never looked upon music as a means to secure celebrity or a life of ease, but rather as an art to which man is dedicated by fate and by which he is enabled to reveal his mind and lay bare his heart.

Ravel did not often "lay bare his heart," but those rare passages which do reveal his inner tenderness have given his music a quality of unexpected enchantment.

For several years following the war Ravel seems to have deliberately concealed this sensitivity, and to have covered it with a hard polished surface of unadorned perfection. His reaction against Schoenberg's atonality to the opposite direction of pure melody was now carried to extreme limits. The duo Sonata for violin and cello—written after *La Valse*—is stripped of every elaboration which could be interpreted as harmonic charm. Everything unnecessary has been ruthlessly eliminated, and only the simplest melody remains.

"Ce bougre de Duo me donne bien du mal," [7] said Ravel in September 1921. The first draft of the Scherzo failed to satisfy him, and he rewrote it entirely. The Sonata has four movements. The first announces the various themes. The second—a Scherzo—is interesting in its development but contains passages that are raucous and not pleasing to the ear (*"colères de chat,"* says Roland-Manuel). The Andante, however, lends itself well to Ravel's new trend toward pure melody; it is full of quiet serenity. In the Finale there is a turbulent exchange of dialogue between the violin and cello. The form of this movement recalls Mozart's sonatas.

The première of Ravel's Sonata for cello and violin was played by the talented cellist Hans Kindler and the violinist Jelly d'Aranyi (to whom Ravel later dedicated *Tzigane*) at the London salon of Mme Alvar. It became very popular in London circles, and was repeated in several homes, including that of Lady Rothermere.

In 1922 the *Revue Musicale* published a special number in honor of Fauré. This venerable composer was now in his seventy-eighth year, and close to the end of his life; he was beloved of all his contemporaries, and many of these contributed touching tributes to the *Revue Musicale's* "Hommage à Gabriel Fauré." Ravel's offering to his old master of Conservatory days, as mentioned in Chapter V, was a charming *Berceuse sur le nom de Gabriel Fauré*, a composition for violin and piano. In the same summer of 1922 Ravel orchestrated Moussorgsky's *Pictures at an Exhibition*.

The year 1924 saw the production of the brilliant virtuoso number for violin called *Tzigane,* originally written with lute accompaniment and later transcribed for orchestra. The first part is a long introduction or recitatif for violin alone—a series of variations such as gypsies love to develop from their native themes, and giving the effect of improvisation. The work begins in slow tempo and gradually increases to a dazzling whirlwind of violin acrobatics. *Tzigane* is seldom played because few have the superlative technique necessary to do it justice.

"Ronsard à son âme," a song written in the same

"THE CHILD AND THE SORCERIES"

year in honor of the French poet Ronsard's four-hundredth anniversary, is a moving epitaph of calm and pure simplicity. The accompaniment in fifths recalls an ancient organ, and the ending of the song fades away in soft chords suggestive of eternal sleep.

Passant, j'ai dit, suis ta fortune,
Ne trouble mon repos: je dors! *

During the early years of the war, Jacques Rouché, director of the Paris Opera, suggested to the noted author Colette (*"la grande debussyiste des lettres"*) that she write a *divertissement féerique* for the stage. After some discussion they decided that Ravel was the composer best suited to set this to music. Accordingly a copy of Mme Colette's book was sent to Ravel at the front. It never reached him, so at the end of the war they approached him again.

The subject of the work could not fail to appeal to Ravel. Fantasy and fairy lore—nature and the world of make-believe and a generous dash of satire—all these things were combined in Colette's work, and brought back to Ravel the days of *Ma Mère l'Oye* and *Shéhéra-zade.* But the original title—"Ballet pour ma fille"— amused him highly. "Why," he exclaimed, "should I write a 'ballet for my daughter'? I have no daughter."

The work was finally called *L'Enfant et les sortilèges* —literally, "The Child and the Sorceries" (sometimes

* Passer-by, I said, follow your fortune,
Do not trouble my repose: I sleep!

195

translated "Dream of a Naughty Boy"). Ravel, although he promised to compose the music for this *divertissement féerique*, did not begin serious work on the score until several years later. The bitterness and depression of the war had first to find release through the violent measures of *La Valse* and the strident themes of the Duo Sonata. In *Tzigane* and in "Ronsard à son âme," Ravel gradually returned to a more normal viewpoint and in 1924 began strenuous work on *L'Enfant et les sortilèges*.

Je ne quitte pas le boulot, ne vois personne, sors juste le temps qu'il faut pour ne pas claquer; si L'Enfant et les sortilèges *ne vient pas à terme, ce ne sera pas de ma faute.** [8]

This *divertissement féerique* was first heard on March 21, 1925, in Monte Carlo. During the two seasons following, it was on the repertoire of the Opéra-Comique but had no great success. The Duet of the Cats was especially criticized. Honegger,[9] however, saw in it "the most extraordinary part of the score. Ravel did not imitate the mewing of cats, but rather used this as the inspiration for his melodic line. The whole problem of so-called 'imitative music' is here."

L'Enfant et les sortilèges was written, said Ravel, "in the spirit of an American operetta." In this composition he returns to his earlier world of fairy-tales, but to it he brings the full development of his powers. Once more—

* I stick to the grind, see no one, go out just often enough to keep from cracking up; if *L'Enfant et les sortilèges* isn't done on time, it won't be my fault.

and for nearly the last time—he allows the tenderness of his nature to be seen; although in curious contrast to this childlike candor a brusque and rebellious sophistication appears in certain parts—in the Cats' Duet, for instance, the amusing fox-trot of the teapot and cup, and the chorus of Arithmetic and his digits. The delightful and whimsical plot would be admirably suited to an animated motion-picture such as Walt Disney has created. When Edouard Ravel saw *Snow White* (a few months after his brother's death), he said: "This is the way *L'Enfant et les sortilèges* should be presented!"

At one of the last appearances of the opera, Ravel noticed that someone in the box next to him was trying (in vain) to whistle by way of showing disapproval. Ravel turned to his friend Roland-Manuel and "discreetly confided to him a key that he happened to have —suggesting that he lend it to the gentleman next door. . . ." [10] Ravel had a keen sense of humor; he could always laugh at his own failures. After reading a particularly unfavorable report of his new operetta he wrote (on his way to Norway): [11] "*L'Enfant,* according to *Le Temps,* seems to me to have received a slap . . ."

The scene of the operetta is an old Norman house. A fire is burning on the hearth, with a tea-kettle singing on the hub and a black cat purring before it. Against the wall stands a large clock, and in the window (its cretonne curtains figured with shepherds and shepherdesses) hangs a cage containing a squirrel. Everything is peaceful—with the exception of a small boy who sits before his lesson books in open rebellion: [12]

> I don't want to do my lessons—
> I want to go out and play;
> I want to eat all the cakes;
> I want to pull the cat's tail,
> And cut off the squirrel's!

His mother, entering with his tea on a tray, scolds him for his laziness. But instead of repenting, the child puts out his tongue at her.

"Oh!!!" exclaims *Maman*, setting down the tray severely. "Here is the *goûter* of a naughty boy: tea without sugar and dry bread. You shall stay alone until dinner time."

As soon as the boy is left alone, he shrieks in a rage:

> *Justement j'ai pas faim;*
> *Justement j'aime mieux rester tout seul;*
> *Je n'aime personne;*
> *Je suis très méchant—*
> > *Méchant—*
> > > *Méchant—*
> > > > *Méchant!*

Then he goes into a tantrum—turns into a little demon of destruction—throws the teapot and cup on the floor, where they break into pieces—tears up his books —climbs onto the window seat and pokes furiously at the squirrel with his pen—pulls the cat's tail—upsets the kettle of water, which falls on the fire with a hissing of steam—and in a final spurt of rage slashes the curtains and yanks out the clock's pendulum.

"Hurrah! Hurrah!" he cries exultantly. "I'm free, free—naughty and free!"

He falls into a chair. But to his amazement it walks away from beneath him, goes over to the armchair, and bows clumsily, saying:

"At last we are free of that terrible child. No more cushions for his slumbers, nor resting place for his dreams. . . ." The two chairs dance together as the child watches them, speechless with wonder. The clock advances from its corner.

> Ding, ding, ding, ding, ding, ding;
> And again ding, ding, ding!
> I can't stop striking!
> I don't know what time it is any more.

Two nasal voices are heard from the floor.

"How's your mug?" says the Wedgwood teapot (in English!).

"Rotten!" answers the Chinese cup (also in English).

The teapot advances towards the child with the threatening gestures of a boxer.

> I punch, sir, I punch your nose,
> I knock you out, stupid chose!
> Black and chic, and vrai beau gosse,
> I box you, I marm'lad' you. . . .

The cup points a vengeful finger at the boy: "Ping-pong, ping-pong, keng-ça-fou, Mah-jong . . . Sessue

Hayakawa. . . ." The cup and the teapot dance a fox-trot together. (This is a masterly take-off on American jazz.)

The child, shivering with fear and cold, draws near to the fireplace. But the fire leaps in his face. "Get back! I warm the good, but I burn the bad!"

Fire rushes after him, but—pursuing the fire and at last conquering his flames—comes the undulating gray shape of Ashes. The child has hardly recovered from his fright when he hears small voices and delicate music approaching from the windows. A procession of miniature shepherds and shepherdesses descends from the torn curtains, lamenting their destruction to the accompaniment of an enchanting melody played by reed-pipes and tambourines.

The child begins to realize what he has done, and starts to cry. All at once from the pages of his torn books a beautiful fairy princess rises:

> I was . . . your first beloved,
> But you have torn the book;
> What will become of me?

The boy tries to hold the lovely vision, but she sinks through his grasp and disappears into the ground. In her place emerges a little old man surrounded by digits from the arithmetic book.

"*Mon Dieu! c'est l'Arithmétique!*"

The digits form a circle and dance about the child while the old man mutters in a high falsetto:

200

Four and four, eighteen—
Eleven and six, twenty-five—
Seven times nine, thirty-three—

"Oh! My head! My head!" cries the tormented child. He is drawn into the midst of the whirling figures, and (to a vigorous chromatic scale) drops to the ground. Night is falling, and there is a long pause.

Then the black cat sees his lady-love in the garden, and jumps to the window ledge. Together they sing a highly amusing duet in cat language. *"Duo miaulé musicalement,"* says the score. (Opinion as to the *musical* merit of this passage is not always unanimous. . . .)

During the "musically miaou-ed *Duo*" the walls of the room gradually recede and the child finds himself in his garden, where a full moon illuminates the trees and flowers with soft radiance.

There follows a scene of pure enchantment. Chorus of tree-frogs—flight of dragonflies, moths, and bats—gambols of squirrels . . . all to the delicate accompaniment of some of Ravel's most inspired music.

But each of the animals has a grudge against the child. He has wounded the squirrel, captured the dragonflies, killed a bat, slashed the trees. . . . They turn on him vengefully. In terror he cries *"Maman! . . ."*

In the confusion of the attack a small squirrel is hurt, and the child, now thoroughly repenting his naughtiness, binds up the animal's wound.

All at once there is silence. The creatures of the garden cannot understand this sudden change in their

201

enemy. He who has always been destructive has now come to the rescue of one of them. Then they discover that the child, too, has been hurt; he is bleeding. What shall they do? they ask each other. *"Que faire . . . nous l'avons blessé—que faire?"* They are powerless to help him—but they remember his call, and all together try to formulate the magical word:

"*Ma . . . man! Ma . . . man!*"

A light appears in the window. Dawn fills the garden with a rosy glow. The nightingale sings and silently the animals disappear.

"*Maman!*" The child holds out his arms to his mother.

"*Il est sage . . . si sage! Il est bon, il est sage!*" sings the departing chorus.

XVI

RAVEL'S HOME AT MONTFORT-L'AMAURY

"LE BELVÉDÈRE" DESCRIBED—RAVEL'S LOVE OF PLAYFUL IMPOSTURE—AS HOST, TEACHER, AND RACONTEUR—HIS SIAMESE CATS—HÉLÈNE JOURDAN-MORHANGE—SONATA FOR VIOLIN AND PIANO

ON a rolling hill that overlooks the beautiful Ile de France country and the forest of Rambouillet lies the picturesque little village of Montfort-l'Amaury. Narrow, cobblestoned streets wind steeply up to the central Place, where an ancient church dreams of centuries gone by. A few shops and a café fronting the old church—with small tables set outside in typical French fashion—are the only modern touches in this medieval village; these, and a few brick and stucco villas whose frivolous architecture shows up in unflattering contrast to the mellowed stone work of the other houses.

One of these villas, ornamented in Baroque style with trimmings of white woodwork, stands at the edge of Montfort-l'Amaury. Nothing distinguishes this house, at least in outward appearance, from hundreds of other French country villas belonging to small tradesmen or

203

country folk of the bourgeoisie. Within, however, it is unique—a perfect expression of a completely individual personality. For this is the home of Maurice Ravel.

Following the death of his mother, Ravel lived for nearly five years with M. and Mme Bonnet and his brother Edouard in St-Cloud, just outside of Paris. He had always longed, however, to have a place of his own, and having discovered that he could work much better in the country, away from the distractions of city life and the too frequent interruptions of well-meaning friends, he decided to find a location which would have all the advantages of country seclusion, and still be within convenient distance of Paris. After spending some time in searching he found, in 1922, just what he had been looking for in the village of Montfort-l'Amaury, about 45 kilometers (28 miles) from Paris.

Ravel's choice of a home was characteristic of his nature. He did not seek an elaborate place; the French countryside is filled with beautiful châteaux surrounded by acres of parks and gardens. But large spaces were alien to Ravel's temperament. With all the countryside to choose from he finally selected a small villa built on a hillside and flanked by a minute garden. Here was exactly what he wanted: the opportunity to create perfection within the security of small limits, refreshment for his soul in the magnificent view over hills and valley which stretched out beneath his windows, and inspiration for his music in the forest of Rambouillet close to his door where he could walk whenever the creative spirit prompted him to solitary communion.

Everything about this place enchanted Ravel. The rooms were microscopical?—just what he desired. Kitchen and plumbing medieval?—all the better; he could modernize them to suit himself. Garden a pocket-handkerchief?—a chance to show what could be done in such narrow dimensions! He was like a child with a new toy; this was his first real home, and his first opportunity to express his own personality and tastes. He planned every detail and did much of the work himself —had the kitchen remodeled with tiled walls and a modern stove, installed a real bathroom with painted tin tub and shower (he was always adding new gadgets)— and in a final outburst of artistic energy he decorated the rooms himself with stenciled designs in black and white. The result of these labors was not unattractive (though certainly unique): an austere combination of Japanese and Grecian with a liberal dash of Empire, Restoration, and Louis-Philippe thrown in. By way of paradox, so dear to his heart, Ravel chose a conventional and somewhat grandiose name for his bandbox of a house. He called it "Le Belvédère."

Le Belvédère still remains, exact in every detail, as Ravel left it in December of 1937 when he went to the private hospital in Paris. Edouard has not allowed a paper to be moved. He wishes to maintain the minute establishment as a memorial to his brother. Mme Reveleau, Ravel's faithful old *bonne* who came to him when he first moved to Montfort-l'Amaury, is there to watch over and care for the cherished possessions of her departed master. She keeps the house filled with flowers from the garden. When she speaks of the quiet little man who was like a child to her during the sad last years of his life, the tears come to her eyes: *"Il était si bon . . .* so easy to care for!" There is an atmosphere of strange expectancy in the little house, as if at any moment a light step might be heard at the door, or the familiar sound of music come drifting from the study at the end of the narrow hall.

The street door of Le Belvédère opens into a small entry facing a diminutive den. The kitchen, resplendent with its white tile (the pride of the village!), is on one side; on the other, the dining-room and balcony overlook the garden. Here are a small table with an extra top to be used when there are guests, an antique wall-fountain, and hangings of dull gold; and on the walls and chimney-place are stenciled designs in geometrical patterns by Ravel's own hand. These decorations are repeated with variations throughout the house.

The tiny salon next to the dining-room is a mixture of Empire and Japanese. Two cupboards filled with china and small objets d'art flank each end of a canapé. These are really secret doors to inner closets which Ravel designed as part of the *imposture* of this room. He loved to astonish his friends. "Cupboards? *Mais non*—they are hidden doors," he would explain, opening them up to show the music closets within.

206

e Reveleàu, Ravel's faithful *bonne,* in the diminutive (but modern)
kitchen ·of Le Belvédère

Le Belvédère, Ravel's villa at Montfort-l'Amaury

After the salon comes a miniature library with a few shelves of rare books, and next to that, down two steps and through a narrow hall, Ravel's own study. This room, where many masterpieces were created, is so restricted in size that an Erard grand piano nearly fills it completely. A small desk and chair and an étagère of bibelots take up the remaining space.

But what a wealth of objects in such limited quarters! Every inch of the piano and shelves is covered with miniature articles—porcelain sofas and doll furniture, a blown-glass ship on painted waves (these waves, to Ravel's delight, could be manipulated to rock the boat), glass ball paper-weights with flower centers, all kinds of small boxes, vases, and lamps, and under a glass dome a gaily dressed doll representing Adélaïde, of ballet fame.

Dearest of Ravel's treasures was a tiny nightingale in a gilded cage which could sing and flutter its little feathered wings. He named it Zizi, and never tired of winding it up and listening to its mechanical warbles. The sculptor Léon Leyritz presented the bird to Ravel one evening at a rehearsal. Tradition has it that the *répétition* was delayed for two hours while the master amused himself with the new toy. . . .[1]

No stranger visiting Ravel's house would suspect that this was the home of a great composer. One sheet of music only is visible in the entire establishment—the Menuet from the *Tombeau de Couperin* on the piano in the little study. Ravel seemed to compose by magic. No one ever saw him at work or found evidence of his labors on his desk or piano. Roland-Manuel says it was "as if the keys of the piano operated directly on the printing press." Ravel's desire to astonish made him compose almost as if in secrecy.

The study is decorated in somber colors—wall-paper of deepest slate gray, and curtains so dark that they look black. Ravel must have found these dark colors soothing to his high-strung nerves; whenever he wanted light and color he had only to look out over the inspiring view of sweeping meadows, orchards, and forest which stretched out before his window.

Ravel's bedroom is on a lower level, opening directly on the terrace of the garden. This contains a Directoire bed, with canopy of gold silk, and a fireplace decorated in his own designs. Everything remains, as in the time of its master, in meticulous and impeccable order.

Just outside of the bedroom is a narrow, graveled terrace, bordered in the spring with yellow pansies; below this is a miniature garden carefully planned and laid out in Japanese style by the master himself. A small pool, flagged walks leading down the hill, clumps of tiny flowers and dwarf trees—all give an illusion of space. Ravel had a special affection for Japanese dwarf trees and for what he called the "concentrated force" of their restricted growth. Achievement within limitation—and even because of it—seemed to him the highest order of accomplishment, and the miniature perfection of the Japanese trees was a symbol of this attainment.

Ravel had a curious predilection for reproductions of reality (*trompe l'œil*) and preferred copies, if well made, to the originals. If an imitation was so successful that it deceived others into believing it to be authentic, this seemed to him more truly art than the real in itself. An artist, he maintained, should be a conscious creator (that is, an interpreter according to his understanding of the actual) rather than merely "sincere," for sincerity from an artistic standpoint implies impulsiveness, or lack of self-control, and is likely, he said, to be no more than a form of indiscretion; whereas consciousness— "artificiality," as he sometimes called it—implies self-control and a transformation of the emotions into art. Man's superiority over the animals, according to Ravel, consists in his ability to counterfeit Nature through the intelligence of his control.

Ravel delighted in showing his "mansion" to the friends who came to visit him. They found his home charming, but at the same time rather childish and somewhat ridiculous, and they often teased him about his execrable *mauvais goût*. "Rococo" and "Baroque" were the mildest of their epithets. Some called Le Belvédère an *intérieur de vieille demoiselle de province;* others said that his study was a "chamber of horrors." Ravel was not disturbed; he only laughed. "But I like it," he insisted; "it suits me!"

He took a childlike pride in the success of the "illusion" of his salon. Nothing pleased him so much as to be able to tell visitors who admired his rare prints and fine porcelains: *"Mais c'est du faux—ça vient des grands magasins!"* * He cherished a ball of smoked crystal on a pedestal in his salon, and pointed it out with such pride that his guests invariably exclaimed in real or pretended admiration. Then he would burst out laughing: "It's nothing but a burned-out electric globe. . . ."

In his pride and joy over Le Belvédère, Ravel was like a gay and naïve child. For a few happy years—after he had recovered from the war's depression and the loss of his mother, and before the tragedy of his later days—he knew a carefree existence. Le Belvédère was mother, wife, and child to him, and through it he found the only real personal expression of his entire life.

Aside from this, music was his only outlet. As a whole, his life was colorless, almost devoid of so-called "human interest"; no violent emotions or overwhelming passions clouded the clear mirror which reflected his art. He was a channel through which music flowed, controlled and guided by his superlative craftsmanship, but unrestricted by the self-limited vision of those who live too intensely personal lives.

Ravel had a strangely detached nature. His attitude towards his own music was as impersonal as if it had been the work of another. He could seldom be persuaded to listen to his own compositions. At concerts he would escape to the corridors for a *"cigarette libératrice."* He was indifferent to success, and the idea of a "career" never occurred to him. The greater the public's acclaim,

* "But it's all imitation—it comes from department stores!"

the more resolutely he clung to simplicity. He made music because he had to (*"comme un pommier fait ses pommes"*), never with a thought of advancing himself or of making money. He was completely unbusinesslike —did not even want his pupils to pay him for their lessons—and made barely enough from his compositions and concerts to live in comfortable but modest style.

Roland-Manuel, Maurice Delage, Manuel Rosenthal (conductor and composer), and Ralph Vaughan Williams were the only real pupils Ravel ever taught. Others, including several young Americans, came to him at various times, but he did little more than criticize their work and give them a few suggestions.

He was always interested in younger musicians—*if* they had talent—and especially if they were making a sincere effort to develop their gifts. "Everyone is talented," he told these youthful artists, and added with characteristic detachment: "I am no more talented than any other—with a little application every one of you could do as well as I have." When they asked for an explanation of some of his compositions he would only shrug his shoulders and smile: "*Je fais des logarithmes* —it is for you to understand them!" He did not want the younger generation to admire his own works too much. "I would rather have you detest them," he said, "than be too much influenced by them." Originality was the most important of all things in his estimation, and he believed that music could live and progress only through the fresh discoveries of the oncoming generation.

As host of Le Belvédère, Ravel was gracious and entertaining. He greeted his friends quietly, but the engaging frankness of his smile and the sparkle of his black eyes spoke more eloquently than the words of welcome which he found himself unable to express. Sunday usually found a crowd of friends at Le Belvédère, and if the weather was fine they lunched on the terrace by the edge of the garden. Jacques de Zogheb, Jacques de Lacretelle, and other neighbors from Montfort-l'Amaury were sure to be there; Colette, who had a country place not far away, occasionally joined the group; there were always some of the Apache clan and one or more interpreters of Ravel's music: Madeleine Grey, Mme Bathori, Marguerite Long, and others. It was at this period that he met Hélène Jourdan-Morhange, the gifted young violinist whom he admired devotedly and whose friendship—especially in his last years—meant so much to him.

All leading musicians of the day found their way at one time or another to the "doll's house" at the top of the hill in Montfort-l'Amaury. There were gay parties with hours of music and of endless discussion. Towards the close of the day Ravel would usually suggest a walk through the forest to the village of Rambouillet—"*pour prendre un petit verre.*"

As a story-teller Maurice Ravel (sometimes called "Rara" by his friends) was clever and amusing; he expressed himself well, with simple elegance and a certain dramatic ability. Everything he did, even to the relating

Maurice Ravel with his Siamese kitten, "Mouni"

At Biarritz (about 1925) with Hélène Jourdan-Morhange and Ricardo Viñes

of anecdotes, was influenced by his desire for perfection. He had an unusual gift for imitation, and could reproduce the calls of birds and animals in a singularly realistic way. If someone paid him a compliment he would try to conceal his pleasure and embarrassment by turning aside with a humorous bird or animal cry. . . .

With Debussy he had a common trait in his passion for cats. Ravel's innate reserve and shyness left him only when he was with children or with animals. A Siamese family shared his quarters at Le Belvédère for several years, and were his chief delight and amusement. The inscrutable natures of these animals, with their unusual intelligence and curious devotion, reminded him, he said, of the Basque temperament. He not only understood cats—he could talk their language. It was perhaps his conversations with the Siamese which gave him the idea for the "Duo of the Cats" in *L'Enfant et les sortilèges*. Often when he was working, his cats would join him and play on his writing table. One day he and Hélène Jourdan-Morhange were amusing themselves by singing together the "Duo des chats" when suddenly the entire Siamese family arrived in greatest consternation. Apparently the music was entirely too realistic. . . . Mouni, one of the kittens, became Mme Jourdan-Morhange's godchild. Ravel was as solicitous over his cats as a hen over her chickens. He exchanged bulletins with his friend:

Bien reçu vos deux cartes, chère Marraine de Mouni. Votre filleul est en forme, mais son frère, à force de s'empiffrer, s'est

213

envoyè une gastrite. Cela ne les empêche pas de jouer à la jongle sur la pelouse. La commission est faite—je vous lêche donc le bout du nez. . . .*

To Hélène Jourdan-Morhange, Ravel dedicated his celebrated Violin Sonata. She was, at that time, one of the most talented of the younger violinists (an injury to her hand later ended a brilliant career), and Ravel took the opportunity to explore, through her knowledge of the instrument, all the resources of the violin. He consulted her frequently about appropriate fingering and bowing, and even sent imperious requests for information: *"Venez vite avec votre violon et les 24 caprices de Paganini,"* he telegraphed one day.

The violin and the piano he considered "essentially incompatible" instruments,† and in the Sonata, instead of trying to blend them, he set himself the problem of bringing out the contrasts between the two.

During his years at Montfort-l'Amaury, Ravel saw a great deal of Hélène Jourdan-Morhange. The two had much in common: music, love of cats, and understanding and respect for each other's temperament. This sympathy, according to many, ripened into something deeper

* Received your two cards, dear Godmother of Mouni. Your godson is in good shape, but his brother has so gorged himself that he is suffering from gastritis. This doesn't prevent them from playing jungle on the lawn. The message is finished—I lick the end of your nose. . . .

† Tchaikowsky, it is said, had the same conviction. He composed only one work for strings and piano—the Trio in A minor, Opus 50 (written, some believe, only because of Mme von Meck's influence).

—at least on Ravel's part, but he was too diffident to express himself unless sure of response. Mme Jourdan-Morhange remained faithful to the memory of her husband, killed in the war, but always stayed close to Ravel in friendship.

XVII

CONCERTS IN AMERICA

IN 1922 Ravel was invited by the renowned French-
American pianist E. Robert Schmitz to become a member of the Consulting Committee of the Franco-American
Society. At that time Ravel was working on his Sonata
for violin and cello; in reply to Mr. Schmitz he wrote:

*Lorsque votre lettre m'est parvenue j'étais en train de ter-
miner—avec quelle fureur!—une Sonate pour V^{lon} et V^{lle} qui
m'a demandé près d'un an et demi de travail. . . . C'est fini
depuis quelques jours; je me suis accordé un permis de con-
valo et, s'il n'est pas trop tard, je viens vous assurer que
j'accepte avec grand plaisir de faire partie du Comité Con-
sultatif de la* Franco-American Society.*

* When your letter reached me I was just completing—with
what fury!—a Sonata for Violin and Cello that has required
nearly a year and a half of work. . . . It was finished a few
days ago; I am allowing myself convalescent leave and, if it is
not too late, I assure you that it will give me pleasure to become
a member of the Consulting Committee of the Franco-American
Society.

The Franco-American Society later developed into Pro Musica—an organization devoted to presenting the contemporary music of all nations, with branch societies in most of the leading American cities. Mr. Schmitz, president of Pro Musica, tried for several years to persuade Ravel to come to the United States and give a series of concerts of his own works under the auspices of this organization; but the French composer always refused. "I am not a pianist," he insisted, and added with characteristically dry humor, "I do not care to be exhibited like a circus."

In 1926 Mr. Schmitz and his wife made a special pilgrimage to Montfort-l'Amaury and tried once more to persuade Ravel. The composer was still uninterested—though this did not prevent his being, as usual, a courteous and affable host. His guests must, he urged, remain at Le Belvédère for lunch (*"Mme Reveleau vous prépare un plat spécial!"*). *Mais non,* they were not interfering with his work. . . .

After lunch the Schmitzes tried again to leave. "But first you must see the garden," Ravel insisted. Finally, having kept them until late afternoon, he decided to drive back with them to Paris, and they all went to the Café de la Paix for an *apéritif*. Here the discussion about the possibilities of an American tour was resumed.

"You would make a fortune in the United States," Schmitz told Ravel.

The latter shrugged his shoulders. *"Peut-être que si, peut-être que non . . ."* he replied.

217

Schmitz made a sudden decision.

"And if I were to guarantee you ten thousand dollars?"

Ravel's eyes opened.

"Ten thousand *dollars*—for a three months' tour? *Mais c'est beaucoup d'argent ça!*"

"Minimum," Schmitz replied. "You might make even more. There are fifteen Pro Musica societies in the United States; we can count on five thousand from them. The rest will follow—I am willing to guarantee the full amount."

Ravel was tempted. After thinking the matter over he finally agreed to come to the United States. Fortunately the Schmitzes, knowing how impractical Ravel was in business matters, thought to question him about other obligations.

"You are sure no one else has a contract for your American appearances?" they asked.

He was a little vague about the matter, but thought not. Daniel Mayer was his manager in England, but surely that would not have anything to do with the United States? Upon investigation it was found that the English contract included "all English-speaking countries."

Mayer, however, was eventually persuaded to relinquish his option on Ravel's American appearance for the sum of $1,000.

The following day Ravel sent the Schmitzes a letter confirming his intention to come to America:

Le Belvédère
Montfort-l'Amaury
29 May, 1926

To M. and Mme E. R. Schmitz
3 Square du Champ de Mars
Paris

Chers Amis,

I confirm to you by the present our conversation of yesterday.

If you succeed in releasing me from the remainder of Daniel Mayer's contract, I authorize you to deal, for North America including Canada, with the manager whom you will choose,* and on the following terms:

I shall receive $10,000 (ten thousand dollars) minimum guarantee for a period of two months (season 1927-1928) in consideration of a number of concerts limited to an average of two a week.

In addition, I agree through this letter to accept no other proposition for these countries [United States and Canada] during the period of option—that is, from June 1, 1926, to February 1, 1927, final date on which I agree to sign a definite contract with you or the representative you may choose, if this contract is *at least equal* to the minimum of ten thousand dollars and with the conditions of restricted time.

It is understood, however, that you will keep me informed as to the progress of this project during its development.

MAURICE RAVEL

The Schmitzes were sure of $5,000 from Pro Musica, but were obliged to arrange for the remainder of the guarantee. Germaine, capable and charming wife of Robert Schmitz, thought of an easy plan to raise this amount. On her return she went to Boston and inter-

* The Bogue-Laberge Bureau in New York City.

viewed the head of the Mason & Hamlin Piano Company.

"Maurice Ravel is coming to the United States next year to appear with Pro Musica," she told him. "Would it be worth something to you if he were to play your piano exclusively while on this tour?"

Now, Paderewski's endorsement had brought millions in trade to the Steinway Company, and all the leading piano manufacturers were anxious to have the recommendation of outstanding artists for their instruments. Henry Mason believed that such an arrangement with Ravel would prove valuable publicity for his firm, and he was willing to sign a contract for $5,000 to have the French musician recommend and play exclusively on the Mason & Hamlin piano.

When all the obstacles to the famous American tour seemed to have been removed, Ravel suddenly remembered an important detail. *"Et mes cigarettes?"* he asked. "You know how I depend on my French Caporals. . . ."

But Ravel smoked prodigious numbers of cigarettes, and it would have cost a fortune in custom duties to bring a three months' supply into the United States. Eventually, therefore, by special arrangement an American firm agreed to manufacture his cigarettes in this country from the same tobacco blend as that used in the French Caporals. It was also arranged that he should have his favorite French wines while traveling.

Ravel left France a few days before the close of 1927, and arrived in New York on January 4, 1928. He did not want his coming made public, but the newspaper reporters were waiting at the dock when he landed. From that moment he found himself the center of an enthusiastic throng of admirers. Telephones and telegrams besieged him at his hotel (the clerk at the desk and Mme Schmitz were busy taking messages and interpreting them)—invitations to lunch, dinner, and tea poured in, and tributes of flowers and letters. All this proved a bewildering experience to the shy, retiring little man. Fortunately his sense of humor saved him from utter confusion, and he found presently—to his own surprise—that he was more flattered than disturbed by so much attention.

Mme Schmitz helped him to unpack, and marveled at his wardrobe. "Maurice Ravel's trousseau was something to shout about," she says. "Twenty pairs of pajamas—dozens of gay shirts and waistcoats—ties galore!" Ravel was in a state because his new evening ties, delivered just before he sailed, were all half an inch too long. Mme Schmitz volunteered to shorten them—there were fifty-seven in all!

Ravel was overwhelmed by the vast skyscrapers and canyon-like streets of New York. He took great delight in walking through the city, window-shopping as he went, especially late at night when the traffic was not quite so bewildering. He always wore—even with his evening clothes—a short, old-fashioned yellow overcoat, a voluminous white wool muffler, and white wool gloves (he could not get used to the cold in the United States); and when he walked down the Avenue in this outfit, says Eva Gauthier, "he stopped traffic!"

Ravel was especially fascinated by the clever mechanical gadgets that he found in the United States, and never ceased to marvel at American plumbing. He carried back a number of new ideas to the sleepy village of Montfort-l'Amaury and installed some of these in Le Belvédère.

The evening he arrived in New York he was taken to Roxy's Theater—another eye-opening experience—and there witnessed a "movie-tone" (new at that time) of Theremin's invention in which music is produced by radio waves controlled by movements of the hands. A few days later Koussevitsky conducted the Boston Symphony Orchestra in a concert at Carnegie Hall and Mrs. Thomas Edison invited Ravel to be her guest of honor at the performance.

Koussevitsky played a number of the French composer's works, and when he had finished he turned to Mrs. Edison's box and with his baton indicated her guest of honor. When the audience discovered that Maurice Ravel was present there was great excitement; they all rose to their feet, clapping, whistling, throwing papers and programs into the air. He stood up and bowed, but this would not satisfy the cheering crowd. Koussevitsky insisted on his coming to the stage, where he was given a moving ovation which lasted ten minutes or more.

Ravel was invited by Koussevitsky to come to Boston and conduct the orchestra at Harvard University on

January 12. (This was Ravel's first official appearance in the United States, since his opening concert in New York was not to be until January 15.) The men of the Boston Symphony Orchestra, it is said, were intrigued beyond words when the French conductor appeared at the first rehearsal in a blue shirt with pale blue suspenders, and at the second wore a pink shirt with braces to match!

Of this concert at Harvard the eminent Boston critic, H. T. Parker, wrote: [1]

The customary "University audience" awaited him. It was aware, however, of an event. A long line of ticket-buyers trailed across the lobby; from the gallery above the stage, where they received places, an amusing rank of young heads and shoulders craned over the rail; for now a conductor-composer was to be seen as well as heard. A wreath of green, set with dark-red roses, hung upon his music-stand. . . .

At a glance Monsieur Ravel betrays himself. As he mounted the steps to the stage, his shoulders stooped, his head bent forward. By these signs know the man who sits often and long at his writing table; the musician who is diligent at the pianoforte. Only as he faced the orchestra or audience was he quite erect. Then, at second glance, appeared his short and slender figure; his tanned and aquiline face—for in a time of motor-cars he also walks; his prominent nose, quick, keen eyes, the grayed hair thick and flat upon his head.

His dress, manner, self-possession stamped him as a man of the world whose profession happens to be composer and—sometimes—conductor of music. At no time did Monsieur Ravel relax his dignity, yet as he threaded through the orchestra on his way to or from the stage, he had a word, a smile, a quick Latin gesture, for this or that musician.

The program at the Cambridge concert included *Le Tombeau de Couperin*, Ravel's transcriptions of Debussy's *Danse* and *Sarabande, Rapsodie espagnole*, "Shéhérazade" (sung by Mme Lisa Roma, who accompanied Ravel on his American tour), and, in conclusion, *La Valse*. This latter made a great impression on the audience, although they were already familiar with the composition; the composer's interpretation gave *La Valse* new meaning and vitality.

Ravel's New York debut on January 15, under the direction of Pro Musica, was held at the Gallo Theater. It proved a great success in spite of the small size of the theater (which also had poor acoustics) and the crowds of people; to Ravel's considerable discomfiture many had to be seated on the stage. Several outstanding artists were on the program, including the violinist Joseph Szigeti, the harpist Salzedo, Arthur Lora, flute, Horace Britt, cello, Henry Leon Leroy, clarinet, and the Hart House Quartet from Canada. First on the program was Ravel's string quartet; next came the *Sonatine* with the composer at the piano (he played as encores *Habanera* and *Pavane pour une Infante défunte*), and he also accompanied Greta Torpadie in "Histoires naturelles" and "Chansons madécasses." The *Introduction and Allegro* for harp with accompaniment of string quartet, flute, and clarinet, closed the concert.

The number that proved most interesting to the audience was the recently completed *Sonata* for violin and piano, interpreted by Ravel and Szigeti. This was not entirely new to the American public, for Myra Hess and Jelly d'Aranyi had played it a few weeks before at a Beethoven Association concert. But the music critics were glad to have an opportunity to study this work more closely. The violin sonata is not easy to understand; curious dissonances—created by writing in two keys at once (the piano part in A flat, while the violin plays in G)—make a combination difficult for the ear to follow. The last movement is in typical "blues" style.

Many listeners were amused at this "popular" touch in a serious composition. But Ravel did not intend to be funny. He believed that jazz was legitimate material for composition, and was surprised that so few American composers had availed themselves of this rich and vital source of inspiration. While Ravel's jazz is based on the music of the Negro orchestras of Paris night clubs, here —as in all his "working on a model"—he transmutes the original into something entirely personal while still retaining the essential flavor of the model.

Jazz, to Ravel, was the most important contribution of modern times to the art of music, and as distinct in its form as Spanish dances, the rhapsodies of Hungary, or Russian folk-songs. He traced the beginnings of jazz back to certain old Scottish melodies, and even alleged that some eighteenth-century French and Italian folk music contains rhythms which are an anticipation of modern jazz. Many different races brought their music to the United States, and just as the American people have developed a distinct national personality by combining different races into a united whole, so music in this country has blended various influences into something entirely original, and not to be despised. Ravel asserted that jazz in the United States is made up of two distinct characteristics: underlying pathos (the voice of the down-trodden Negro slaves, plus a hidden yearning for an ideal which Americans themselves hardly understand), and the arrogant will-to-power of a new people rising to world dominion.

In writing of Ravel's concert for Pro Musica at the Gallo Theater, Olin Downes, distinguished critic of the New York *Times,* said: [2]

Mr. Ravel would not profess to be a piano virtuoso. What he did was to distinguish the concert with his presence, and, as a pianist, to present clear expositions of his music. . . . The precision and the taste of his workmanship, the complete technical mastery of his medium, the care with which each different musical idea was worked out complete, impeccable in form and style, were striking manifestations of the art of a composer whose works rebuke the pretense and dilettantism so fashionable in many quarters of Paris today. . . .

Nothing could have been more typical of the precision, economy and refinement of this music than the slight, aristocratic, gray-haired and self-contained gentleman who bore himself with such simplicity on the platform; presenting his music with a characteristic reticence and modesty; well content, as it were, to give an accounting of what he had done, and to leave his listeners to their own conclusions. And, indeed, his achievement speaks for itself.

Never to have composed in undue haste; never to have offered the public a piece of unfinished work; to have experienced life as an observant and keenly interested beholder, and to have fashioned certain of its elements into exquisite shapes of art that embody the essence of certain French traditions, is a goal worth the gaining.

Following the Pro Musica concert Ravel was entertained at an elaborate affair given in his honor by Mrs. Cobina Wright. Mrs. Wright's parties were famous at that time in New York musical and literary circles. She invited several hundred guests to meet Ravel, including critics, patrons of the Philharmonic, Walter Damrosch, Heifetz, and Chaliapin and other singers from the Metropolitan. Knowing Ravel's interest in jazz, Mrs. Wright engaged Hall Johnson and his seventeen Negro Jubilee singers and dancers to entertain the company for an hour or more before the supper.

An incident occurred soon after Ravel came to the United States that is possibly responsible for the report that he was of Jewish origin—a report that is still repeated occasionally. After his second concert in New York, several people came up to congratulate him. "Of course you are Jewish?" one of them asked. Ravel did not at first understand, but when the words were translated, he replied: "From a religious standpoint I am not Jewish, since I have no religion; nor from a racial standpoint, because I am a Basque."

"What are Basques?" he was asked.

"That would be difficult to say," Ravel answered with a smile. "The Basques are of unknown race; no one knows whence they sprang. They look like gypsies and

227

have nomad tendencies, but for many centuries now they have been settled in the south of France." To his friends Ravel added: "I should not mind being Jewish [*si j'étais juif je m'en ficherais*], but I am not!"

The Mason & Hamlin Company not only provided a piano for Ravel's use at his hotel, and another for his tour, but also sent him a piano-tuner capable of acting as courier, interpreter, and general assistant. This versatile person was to join the French composer on the Twentieth Century Limited when he left New York for Chicago; but at the last minute, an unexpectedly severe snowstorm delayed the piano-tuner and he missed the train. Ravel had been invited that day to a luncheon given for him by Paul Kochansky, the Polish violinist, at which a number of his close friends were present, and as usual he lost all count of time. Ravel also would have missed the train if his friends had not suddenly noticed the hour and rushed him to the station. They arrived just in time to get him on board, and not until the train was pulling out did they discover that the indispensable tuner-interpreter-courier was not on the train.

Consternation! What should be done?—for Maurice Ravel spoke no word of English—he could not even order a meal by himself. His friends hurried to the station-master and explained the predicament. The latter was not very resourceful, but finally through Mrs. Edison's influence everything was satisfactorily adjusted. A long-distance call to Albany brought an interpreter to the train at that station, and arranged to have him travel as far as Chicago. Meanwhile a telegram to the conductor ordered Ravel's dinner: "lamb chops, string beans, and coffee. . . ."

In Chicago—as in most of the places he visited—more fêting, more enthusiastic crowds, more wining and dining. There he again met Adolf Bolm and his wife; Bolm was the dancer who had created the role of Dorcon in *Daphnis and Chloe*. Eager to make Ravel's visit as pleasant as possible, the Bolms asked him what he most wanted to see or do. He replied that he would like to visit one of the elegant homes on the North Shore.

One of Chicago's social leaders was delighted to have the celebrated French composer as her guest. She planned an elaborate luncheon, served by numerous butlers and footmen and including every delicacy from lobster to squab. Ravel, however, scarcely touched his food, and his conversation languished with each course. When lunch was over he pleaded a headache, and with courteous bows and thanks departed from the palatial residence.

"*Pour l'amour de Dieu*, stop at the nearest *pharmacie*," he begged the friends who had brought him, "and telephone the hotel to prepare a good meal for me."

"A meal?" his friends replied wonderingly. "But you have just lunched. . . ."

"You call *that* a meal?" Ravel answered peevishly. "There wasn't a thing anyone could eat. No meat at all . . . *mais tout le monde sait que je suis carnivore*," he added, like a child who cannot understand why all the world does not know his idiosyncrasies.

All the seats in the big Auditorium were filled on the night when Ravel was to conduct the Chicago Symphony Orchestra. The audience waited with eager anticipation to hear the famous French composer. The members of the orchestra took their places. Everybody was ready, expectant. But the conductor's stand remained vacant. Ten minutes—fifteen—twenty. Finally, at a few minutes before nine, a somewhat nervous but smiling little man in faultless evening dress made his bow to the audience. Few knew the harrowing tale of his delay. This is what had happened:

Just as Ravel was dressing for the concert he discovered that his evening shoes had been left in one of the trunks at the station. This was a major calamity. Wear his day shoes? *Jamais de la vie!* Maurice Ravel must be correctly—impeccably—dressed or he would not appear in public.

In desperation Mme Roma, the singer who was interpreting his songs, offered to go to the station and unpack the indispensable shoes. She dashed down in a taxi—rummaged through the trunks—back to the Auditorium! —the evening was saved.

Ravel played thirty-one times in the United States, five of his concerts being in New York. He was guest conductor with a number of symphony orchestras, including those of Boston, New York, San Francisco, and Cleveland; and he appeared with Pro Musica in Philadelphia, Detroit, St. Louis, Kansas City, Houston, St. Paul, Denver, Portland, Seattle, Vancouver, and Los Angeles.

Southern California appealed to him especially. He was entertained in Hollywood and taken to visit the moving-picture studios, where he was photographed with John Barrymore and Douglas Fairbanks, Senior. Ravel admired the flowers and palm trees; he wrote to Hélène Jourdan-Morhange:

*10/2/28. Bien reçu vos nouvelles à Los Angeles. 35° à 40° [Centigrade]. Palmiers, plantes de serre bordent les avenues. . . . Je vois des villes magnifiques, des pays enchanteurs, mais les triomphes sont fatigants. A Los Angeles j'ai lâché les gens, d'ailleurs je mourrais de faim.**

Ravel was sorry to leave the warmth of the south. On his trip back to New York he wrote again to Mme Jourdan-Morhange:

29/2/28 . . . Après être sorti à Los Angeles en vêtements de plage, et trouvé partout un temps délicieusement doux, voici le grand froid, la neige, le vent. Demain matin je rentre chez moi à New York . . . Je ne me repose que dans le train— dormi la nuit dernière, et aujourd'hui avant et après le dé-jeuner.†

* 10/2/28. Received word from you in Los Angeles. 35° to 40° [Centigrade]. Palm-trees, hot-house plants border the avenues. . . . I am seeing magnificent cities, enchanting country, but triumphs are fatiguing. In Los Angeles I ran away from the people; besides, I was dying of hunger.

† After going out in Los Angeles in beach clothes, and finding a delightfully mild climate, here is bitter cold, snow, wind. Tomorrow I shall be back in New York . . . I can rest only in the train—slept last night, and today both before and after lunch.

CONCERTS IN AMERICA

Ravel was back in New York on his fifty-third birthday, April 7, 1928, and was given a dinner party (with plenty of red meat!) by the singer Eva Gauthier. She invited George Gershwin, knowing that Ravel greatly admired the American composer's flair for rhythm and his originality in developing jazz themes. Gershwin played the famous *Rhapsody in Blue* and a number of his other compositions, so intricate in rhythm that Ravel was overcome with wonder. Gershwin wanted to study with the French composer, but the latter discouraged him. "You might lose that great melodic spontaneity and write bad Ravel," he told the young American.

Ravel carried away happy memories of his visit to the United States and the warm hospitality of his American friends. Before sailing on the *Paris* the latter part of April, he sent a message of farewell to Germaine Schmitz. It was written on a postcard decorated with a spray of blue flowers:

Le beau bleu de cette fleur, qui ressemble à celui d'un ciel sans nuages, est l'emblême d'un sentiment tendre et délicat qui se nourrit d'espérances. . . .

P. P. C.

MAURICE RAVEL *

And this from the man whom so many considered unsentimental, ironical, cold!

* The lovely blue of this flower, which resembles that of a cloudless sky, is the emblem of a fond and tender feeling which lives on hope. . . .

P. P. C. [To take farewell]

MAURICE RAVEL

XVIII

LAST COMPOSITIONS

"CHANSONS MADÉCASSES"—RAVEL AS A FRIEND
—HIS REACTION TO SUCCESS—LOVE OF NIGHT
LIFE—THE TWO PIANO CONCERTOS—HIS TRIP
TO VIENNA—"DON QUICHOTTE À DULCINÉE"

IN 1925 Hans Kindler, who a few years later became conductor of the National Orchestra in Washington, D. C., suggested to Mrs. Coolidge that she ask Ravel to write a composition for her chamber-music concerts.

The name of Elizabeth Sprague Coolidge has become famous and beloved, both in America and abroad. Because of her great interest in chamber music she has established a Musical Foundation which each year sponsors a series of free concerts throughout the United States. Public libraries, universities, and colleges have been privileged to hear the finest chamber music presented by outstanding string ensembles. Mrs. Coolidge has had an incalculable influence in developing the cultural life of her country both through her generous support of music and through the encouragement she has given younger composers, much of the music played at

233

her concerts having been commissioned by Mrs. Coolidge herself.

Ravel accepted Mrs. Coolidge's commission, and composed a novel form of quartet using the voice as the principal instrument supported by cello, flute, and piano. He had recently become interested in a collection of native Madagascan poems translated into French by Evariste Parny, and chose three of these (the fifth, eighth, and twelfth): "Nadanhove," "Aoua," and "Il est doux."

"Trois Chansons madécasses" is another example of Ravel's ability to identify himself with the subject he seeks to interpret. In this case it is his own inner rebellion that expresses itself when the downtrodden natives sing of their resentment, and the music he composed is, in spite of a certain barbaric irony, a dramatic revelation of human suffering. Ravel considered this one of his finest works (with "Shéhérazade" it was his favorite, according to Edouard Ravel), but it is seldom performed. The singer's part is exacting and ungrateful, and each of the instruments requires the interpretation of a solo artist to do it justice. "This work," says Arthur Hoérée, "is one of the most unusual and valuable in all contemporary music."

Mrs. Coolidge planned a gala première for Ravel's "Chansons madécasses" at the Hotel Majestic in Paris, in October of 1925. This was an invitation affair attended by all the important musicians and critics. Ravel himself was at the piano, Mme Bathori sang, Kindler played the cello, and Fleury the flute. But when the date of the concert arrived Ravel (*comme toujours, en retard*) had completed but one of the songs—the middle number, called "Aoua."

"Aoua" is a pæan of revolt against slavery and the tyranny of the white race. It begins with a wild cry of rebellion:

"Aoua, Aoua! Mistrust the whites, O dwellers of the waterside!"

The strange rhythm has a menacing undercurrent, emphasized by an effect of tomtoms rendered by the piano. After warning the natives against the tyranny of the white race the song ends with the words: "We shall live free. . . ."

France at this time was having trouble with her provinces in Morocco, and war had been declared against the natives. One of the members of Mrs. Coolidge's audience took violent exception to Ravel's song. When, after repeated calls, the artists decided to play the work a second time, the gentleman in question rose from his seat and exclaimed in a loud voice: "*Monsieur L— M— s'en va.* He does not wish to listen again to such words while our country is fighting in Morocco!"

Several of the audience agreed with him. "*Bravo— très bien! Je suis de votre avis. . . .*" ("*Eh bien pas moi!*") But others were indignant at this ill-mannered interruption. "*Mais nous sommes invités!*" "*Vous n'avez qu'à vous en aller. . . .*" ("*A la porte!*") "*Imbé-*

235

cile!" *"Imbécile vous-même!"* (*"Monsieur! Monsieur!"*) *"Bravo M—!"* *"Bravo Ravel . . . !"*

The guest who had started this riot finally withdrew with a small group of sympathizers, and "Aoua" was repeated and enthusiastically applauded. All through the excitement Ravel as usual sat quietly at the piano, and the result of the affair was merely to increase his popularity and the success of the "Chansons madécasses."

The other two songs were not completed until the following year. "Nadanhove," the first of the group, contains a voluptuous, erotic element, and in this respect is unique in the repertoire of Ravel's work. It tells of the beautiful Nadanhove whose kisses penetrate to the soul of her lover. The rhythm, in the form of a berceuse, is syncopated; first comes a long recitation with cello obbligato in contrapuntal style, and later the flute and the piano take up the accompaniment. The last words of the song are:

Tu pars, et je vais languir dans les regrets et les désirs,
Je languirai jusqu'au soir;
*Tu reviendras ce soir, Nadanhove, oh belle Nadanhove! ***

The warlike "Aoua" is second; third and last comes *"Il est doux de se coucher durant la chaleur."* This calm nocturne sings of the peace of evening. "It is pleasant . . . to stretch out beneath a leafy tree and await the re-

---

* You leave me, and I shall languish in regret and desire,
  I shall languish until evening;
  You will return this evening, Nadanhove, O beautiful Nadanhove!

freshing breeze of evening." The beginning is a dialogue between flute and voice; there are gonglike passages in the piano, and the cello plays pizzicato, imitating an African drum. The song dies away as the voice sings:

Le vent du soir se lève; la lune commence à briller au travers des arbres de la montagne.
*Allez, et préparez le repas.**

In 1927 Ravel set to music a poem by his friend Léon-Paul Fargue called "Rêves." It is in much the same style as the "Chansons madécasses." The accompaniment is in three-part counterpoint, with occasional chords and a dreamlike quality that gives the song an effect of transparent simplicity. *Fanfare* was written in the same year, as a prelude to a child's ballet called *L'Eventail de Jeanne*. The score bears the ironical inscription "*Wagneramente*," and Roland-Manuel calls it "a lilliputian flourish of trumpets which begins like the chiming of insect horns and ends in the style of *Götterdämmerung*."

When Ravel returned from the United States in the spring of 1928, a group of his most intimate friends, including his brother Edouard, Mme Bonnet, Maurice Delage and his wife, and Hélène Jourdan-Morhange, came down to Le Havre to meet his boat. Mme Jourdan-Morhange presented him with a stiff bouquet surrounded with lace paper.

---

* The evening breeze rises; the moon begins to shine through the trees on the mountain.
Go, and prepare the repast.

"It was nice of us to come to meet you, wasn't it?" she asked laughingly.

Ravel was outraged. "I certainly would like to have seen you *not* come!" he retorted.

This remark is typical of his nature. Although he made little outward protestation of friendship, actually his friends were infinitely dear to him. He was devoted to them, yet with the tyranny and exaction of a spoiled child. *"Je suis jaloux en amitié,"* he himself confessed. He demanded much of those who were close to him, but in return gave a great deal in his own quiet and unobtrusive way; it almost seemed as if he were ashamed to have his friends suspect how much they meant to him. He was, says Roland-Manuel, the most social of beings, and the least communicative. "The most simple, the most tender, and the most exacting of friends. By his exterior appearance, by his whims, his love of paradox, he contributed to the legend of 'spiritual coldness.' But in spite of these appearances this great 'prisoner of perfection' hid a sensitive and passionate soul which the slightest blow sufficed to wound. *Il ne s'agit pas de s'ouvrir la poitrine pour faire voir qu'on a du cœur. . . ."*

Ravel loved to surprise his friends with unexpected trifles; he was assiduous in secret, small attentions, and like a child would give the things he himself preferred to receive: trinkets, small objects in porcelain, toys, and so on. Returning from a trip to Venice, he presented the ladies of his acquaintance with gaudy belt-buckles of imitation jewels. *"Dieu, que c'est laid!"* one of them exclaimed, and added, ". . . *et que Ravel est gentil!*" Edouard recalls that once, when he himself was ill in a Paris hospital, Maurice, anxious to distract his brother from his sufferings, brought him a mechanical Basque pelota player and placed it on the pillow beside the patient's head. . . .

A few months after his return from America Ravel wrote his famous *Bolero,* and following the dazzling success of this masterpiece he was more in demand than ever. But in spite of his triumphs he remained simple and unspoiled. To a friend who complimented him on his success, saying, *"Bravo, Ravel, c'est la gloire!"* he replied with an ironical shrug of the shoulders, *"Oh! c'est la mode, simplement!"*

Invitations to conduct, to be the honored guest of various European musical festivals, and to receive degrees from several foreign universities were showered on him from every side. Although he refused on three different occasions the French Legion of Honor, he did accept decorations from several other countries, including Belgium and the United States. In 1931 Oxford University conferred on him the degree of *Doctor Honoris Causa.*

His constant travels and the fatigue and excitement of so many public appearances proved too much of a strain on Ravel's none too robust physique, and soon after he returned from America he began to complain of intense weariness and fatigue, and of increasing sleeplessness. His friends urged him to reform his habits—to smoke less and spend reasonable hours in rest. "But why should

I waste my nights in sleep? Night is the time when I plan my work," he insisted, with the fretfulness of a child.

Ravel had always been addicted to the genial French custom of spending leisurely hours at a sidewalk café, with a *petit verre* and an entertaining companion or two; but as the years went on and his insomnia grew worse, such simple relaxation no longer sufficed. When Paris discovered jazz, night clubs began to spring up in every quarter, and Ravel became infatuated with these gay centers of amusement. Now he sought escape from all solitude; the bright lights, the infectious rhythm of the music, and the entertaining company helped him to elude the depression which he could not shake off save in these glittering surroundings.

The "Bœuf sur le Toit" and the "Grand Ecart" were his favorites among the *boîtes de nuit*. The more crowded they were, the denser the smoke and noisier the music, the better he liked it. In the small hours of the morning one of his companions would suggest that it was time to leave. But not Ravel. . . . *"Partir déjà?"* he would exclaim, with a smile that hid his dread of facing alone the remaining hours of the night. *"Pourquoi donc? Mais on s'amuse follement. . . ."*

M. and Mme Bonnet decided about this time to leave St-Cloud and build a house at Levallois-Perret, next door to the factory which Edouard still maintained. An apartment for Maurice was reserved on the second floor of this *hôtel particulier*, and his friend Léon Leyritz designed— in complete contrast to Le Belvédère—an ultramodern

A later portrait of
Maurice Ravel

At St-Jean-de-Luz with
Mme Marguerite Long

Photograph by Jean
Dufour

Ravel returns from the United States. Beside him stands Mme Jou
Morhange. His brother Edouard is on the extreme right.

setting for these rooms, with built-in bed, indirect light-
ing, and a small bar in one corner. Whenever Ravel came
to the city (and during these restless years he would take
the little autobus from Montfort-l'Amaury to Paris several times a week) he stayed with his brother and the
Bonnets at number 17-bis, rue Chevallier. His suite of
rooms has been kept just as he left it. Here, in addition
to the bust by Léon Leyritz, Edouard cherishes Ravel's
death mask and a touching bronze replica of his hand.

The triumphs of his American tour led Maurice Ravel
to consider a second visit to this country, and he decided
to compose a piano concerto to play himself with the
leading American orchestras. Just as he was beginning
this project, an Austrian pianist named Paul Wittgenstein, who had lost his right arm in the war, asked Ravel
to compose for him a work for the left hand alone. Ravel
agreed to do this, and the two piano concertos—so completely different in style and character—were produced
at the same time.

Ravel, in discussing these compositions,[1] said:

It was an interesting experiment to conceive and to realize
simultaneously the two Concertos. The first, in which I shall
figure as executant, is a concerto in the most exact sense of
the term, and is written in the spirit of Mozart and Saint-
Saëns. I believe that the music of a concerto can be gay and
brilliant, and that it need not pretend to depths nor aim at
dramatic effects. . . .

At the beginning I thought of naming the work a *Divertissement*; but I reflected that this was not necessary, the title
"Concerto" explaining the character of the music sufficiently.

From a certain viewpoint my Concerto has some resemblances to the Violin Sonata. It includes some elements borrowed from jazz, but only in moderation.

The Concerto for the left hand alone is of a rather different character and in one movement only, with many jazz effects, and the writing is not so simple.

In a work of this kind it is essential to create the effect not of light, delicate texture, but of a partition written for both hands. . . .

Ravel was many months working on these two compositions. His health growing worse rather than better, he abandoned the idea of himself playing the Concerto in G (as the one for two hands is called) and asked Mme Marguerite Long to take his place in introducing the new work. He dedicated the Concerto to her and she played the première at a brilliant performance in the new Salle Pleyel on January 14, 1932. Ravel conducted the Lamoureux Orchestra to a packed house of 3,500, while hundreds of others were turned away.

A few days after this concert, Mme Long left with Ravel for an extended concert tour through Germany, Poland, Austria, Belgium, Switzerland, Holland, and Rumania, he to direct the orchestras of these countries and she to interpret the new Concerto. Mme Long speaks of Ravel's "legendary abstractedness" while traveling. At every stage of the journey he forgot his baggage, or lost his railroad ticket, or his watch, or kept his mail (or hers) unopened in his pocket—which often caused exciting complications. ("We are accumulating souvenirs," she said ruefully.) But Ravel's good nature never forsook him—he only laughed at his own absent-mindedness.

In Prague he wanted to buy a crystal bottle of a certain form to present to Maurice Delage's mother, who had been his *marraine* during the war. Although they were playing a concert that evening, he was not content until he had searched in every shop and worn himself out—as well as his companion. Months later Mme Long discovered, in his home, the package containing the bottle—still unopened! He had completely forgotten to present it to his *marraine de guerre.*

The Concerto in G is more typical of Ravel than the one for left hand alone—*"plus Ravel,"* as he himself expressed it. He did not wish to make a dramatic or formal affair of this number. On the contrary, he wished it to be, as he said, a *"divertissement"*—gay, sparkling, and ironical, but most of all amusing. The middle part, however, is more than these; this movement is filled with grace, tenderness, and simple melody in striking contrast to the restlessness of the outside movements.

Ravel stated that this second part of his Concerto in G was modeled after a Mozart quintet. It is filled with classical serenity and embodies the philosophy of Ravel's more peaceful moments. "Let us accept what life sends us," he seems to say, "for in acceptance comes beauty—and repose."

The Concerto in G begins with a bright and elegant theme for piccolo. Throughout the work the orchestra is spirited and translucent, and the showering trills and arpeggios of piano and harp recall passages in *Ondine* and *Jeux d'eau*. The presto finale, with its ironical sallies into jazz, is a mad race between piano and orchestra, and here, as throughout the composition, the soloist's part is exceptionally exacting, requiring a combination of superlative technique and, in the middle part, great understanding and depth of feeling.

In none of his compositions is Ravel more completely master of his art than in this concerto. It has been said to embrace all the essentials of his music: brilliance, clarity, elegance, originality; tenderness and simplicity in the middle part, and, in the last movement, daring vigor and brittle perfection.

The left-hand Concerto is a complete contrast to this. Though some consider it one of Ravel's greatest masterpieces, a number of critics feel that it is inferior to the two-handed Concerto. Dominique Sordet says that it is "a witness to the pathetic struggle which had already been declared between [Ravel's] creative intelligence and implacable disease." Other critics call it a *tour de force*—one of those *gageures* or difficult problems which Ravel loved to wrestle with and conquer.

The word *gageure* is constantly associated with Ravel. Literally translated, it means "wager" or "bet." In Ravel's case it meant a bet he made with himself—a hard nut (musically speaking) which he was determined to crack; and the harder it was the better he liked it. In this sense the famous *Bolero* was a *gageure*—a wager with himself that he could make an entire composition

244

out of one theme and a single modulation. The Concerto for left hand was a *gageure* that he could make one hand (the weaker of the pair!) sound like two.

That he succeeded in extraordinary fashion is evident to all who have heard this work. It is hard to believe that one hand alone can create such a full and rich effect— almost, in places, like a whole orchestra by itself. It is written all in one movement, beginning with a muffled introduction of basses and cellos (*brouillard sonore*) to which the other instruments of the orchestra add a crescendo of anguished and fierce intensity; the principal theme is a lugubrious and morose *Sarabande.* The piano begins with fortissimo chords and maintains, throughout the Concerto, a harsh, savage rhythm. Henri Gil-Marchex compares this work to the robust allegros of Bach's *Brandenburg* Concertos interpreted in modern jazz form. The ending he calls a *"ricanement diabolique."*

The *Concerto pour la main gauche* demands a technique of colossal virtuosity, and it is not surprising that Wittgenstein found some of the passages too much for him and was obliged to alter these to suit his ability. Ravel, however, felt that the Austrian pianist had taken unpardonable liberties with his composition. In looking about for someone to play the concerto as he himself wished it performed, he found an able and sympathetic interpreter in Jacques Février, the son of an old comrade of Conservatory days. Henri Février is today a leader in musical and literary circles of Paris, and his son has made a name for himself as one of the most brilliant and talented of the younger pianists. Trained at the Conservatoire under Mme Marguerite Long, Jacques had always been closely associated with Ravel, and now the latter chose him as official interpreter of the Concerto for left hand; he coached him personally in the exact way it should be played. In November of 1937 Février was invited to play the Concerto with Koussevitsky's orchestra in Boston, and there received enthusiastic acclaim. It was just before Jacques Février's departure for the United States—two months before the composer's death—that Ravel's last photograph was taken: in October 1937.

In the fall of 1932, after the long tour through central Europe, Ravel was approached by a motion-picture company and asked to write some music for a film of Don Quixote, which they said was to feature Chaliapin in the title role. Ravel did not know then that several other composers, including Manuel de Falla, Jacques Ibert, and Darius Milhaud, had also been asked to contribute to the musical score.

For this film Ravel wrote three songs called "Don Quichotte à Dulcinée," but they were never accepted. As usual, he was late in completing them, and the film company seized on this as a pretext for refusal; another reason alleged was that Chaliapin did not find the songs sufficiently brilliant in effect.

"Don Quichotte à Dulcinée," Ravel's last composition,

is developed from Spanish and Basque themes. The first song, "Chanson romantique," has an accompaniment that recalls the strumming of a guitar; while the second of the group, "Chanson épique," is a prayer to the Madonna:

> *L'ange qui veille sur ma veille,*
> *Ma douce dame si pareille à vous,*
> *Madame au bleu mantel!*
> > *Amen!*

"Chanson à boire" is a joyous serenade with a strongly marked Spanish *jota* rhythm, full of humor and lyrical audacity. Considering the tragic days which were to follow for Ravel, this song, which is his farewell to music, ends on a strangely ironical note:

> *Je bois à la joie. . . .*

XIX

"SIMPLE, SANS REMORDS"

RAVEL'S ACCIDENT—HIS DECLINING HEALTH—
TWO COMPOSITIONS PROJECTED—TRIP TO SPAIN
AND MOROCCO—THE DIAGNOSIS OF HIS DISEASE,
AND ITS TRAGEDY—HIS OPERATION AND DEATH

IN the fall of 1932 Ravel was badly shaken by a minor
taxi accident in Paris. At the time, the blow on his head
seemed hardly serious, though some of his friends believe he may have suffered an internal injury to the
brain which precipitated his fatal last illness, or at least
that the accident may have hastened the development of
the strange malady which gradually, and by slow degrees, carried him away from the world of the living.

During the next few months, his depression and ex-
haustion became alarming. In the summer of 1933,
while at St-Jean-de-Luz, he suddenly discovered that he
was incapable of making the movements necessary for
swimming. Certain familiar gestures no longer re-
sponded to his command—something strange was hap-
pening to his powers of co-ordination.

Then he discovered that occasionally he had trouble
in speaking. The words with which he wished to interpret

his thoughts no longer came to him readily, like the obedient servants of his consciousness which they had always previously been. His mind remained clear, but the means of expression seemed disconnected. Most tragic of all, he found increasing difficulty in putting his musical thoughts on paper. In time, he could not even sign his name.

These complications did not come upon him all at once. The disease was so gradual in its development that at the beginning he attributed the trouble to fatigue, and felt sure that when his health improved he would regain his former lucidity and co-ordination. In a moment of respite he even started two new works. Mme Ida Rubinstein wanted him to write a new ballet for her, and he suggested a sumptuous dramatization of the *Arabian Nights* legend of Ali Baba and the Forty Thieves, to be called *Morgiane*. He also wanted to write an epic musical poem on the life of Jeanne d'Arc. Ravel was full of musical ideas that clamored for expression; but to write these down was another matter.

He grew more and more distressed over the inexplicable and apparently uncontrollable affliction that paralyzed his faculties; but he never complained, and his brother and the Bonnets did not at first suspect how deeply anxious he felt. Often in the past when he had been questioned about his work he had replied: "It is all finished—only setting it down on paper remains"— and then perhaps months would go by before he did the actual writing. Therefore, when they inquired about

249

the progress of *Jeanne d'Arc* and he replied, "I have it all in my head," they did not realize that now it was literally impossible for him to write it out.

"I shall make a new dress for the première of your *Jeanne d'Arc*," Mme Bonnet said one day. "Hurry and finish the work, for I need the dress!"

Ravel looked at her with a somber expression. "You had better not wait for *Jeanne d'Arc*. God knows whether you or I will ever see that work performed. . . ."

In 1934 he was appointed director of the American Conservatory of Music at the Palace of Fontainebleau, but his failing health prevented much active association with that institution. In 1935 it was decided that a trip to the South might help to distract him. As he had always wanted to see Morocco, in February of that year he and his friend Léon Leyritz started on a tour of Spain and Northern Africa. He seemed at the time to be benefited by the trip. They visited Tangiers and Marrakech, Mamounia and Fez. Here Ravel found the settings he had dreamed of for his *Morgiane;* Morocco was filled with the color, light, and seductive rhythms of the Orient. He who had spoken in the musical idiom of so many different races now wanted to write an Arabian composition. "Only," he said, with a touch of his old malice, *"ce serait beaucoup plus arabe que tout ça. . . ."*

Ravel had an extraordinary gift for assimilating the rhythmical language of the various countries whose music he admired, and for reproducing this in entirely individual fashion in his own works. In *Tzigane* he identifies himself with the gypsy personality; and his Hebrew songs are so imbued with the spirit of that race that this may have been partly responsible for the legend which was circulated about his Jewish origin.

The summer of 1935 found him again at St-Jean-de-Luz, still trying to escape his depression by staying constantly in the society of friends and spending the evenings at concerts or theater. He never spoke of the inner distress that tormented him, and strangers noticed only that he was exceptionally quiet and reserved.

One warm summer's day his friends took him on an expedition into the mountains above St-Jean-de-Luz. Ravel seemed more taciturn and weary than usual, and when they entered a small inn to rest and quench their thirst he sat silently contemplating the magnificent panorama of snow-covered mountains with mournful dejection. Suddenly the strains of *Bolero* sounded from the back of the tavern. Ravel's face lit up . . . he rose swiftly to his feet, *"cherchant la source des sonorités qui demeurent maintenant son unique joie."* He found in a corner a *"méchant phonographe,"* scratchy and out of tune, but it brought to him an unexpected echo of his glory and past labors.[1]

Ravel hoped until the last that the doctors would find some remedy for his trouble. But it was difficult for them to make a diagnosis; some believed he had a tumor of the brain (his later operation proved that this was not true); others called it apraxia or dysphasia. *Affaissement du cerveau* (shrinking of the brain) was the final

251

verdict. Though all these involve certain brain centers that effect muscular co-ordination, these diseases do not in any way impair the reason. Contrary to the rumors which have been so frequently circulated, particularly in the United States, Ravel never lost his mind; far from this, he was pathetically conscious of his own condition.

In the summer of 1937, just a few months before his death, the Orchestre National gave a gala performance of *Daphnis and Chloe*, under the direction of an old Apache, Inghelbrecht. When the concert was ended Ravel took Mme Jourdan-Morhange by the arm and hurried away from the crowds who wanted to congratulate him. In the car he began to weep.

"*J'ai encore tant de musique dans ma tête,*" he said piteously.

She tried to console him and tell him that his work was already complete. But he replied in heartbroken accents:

"*Je n'ai rien dit—j'ai tout à dire encore. . . .*"

Although he had great difficulty in finding words with which to express himself, those who were close to him could follow his thoughts and realize that behind the pitiful impediment of his affliction his reason remained unimpaired. There were frequent proofs—even to outsiders—that this inner intelligence still functioned. Shortly before his death Ravel visited Madeleine Grey and heard her sing his "Don Quichotte à Dulcinée." When she had finished she asked him what he thought of her interpretation. He seemed far away, and she won-

252

dered if he had heard her question; then, suddenly turning to the music on the keyboard, Ravel indicated a
passage which she had somewhat altered from the original, and in halting words tried to explain his reason for
wishing it to be sung exactly as he had written it.
Madeleine Grey says that she mentions this incident in
order that singers may realize how carefully Ravel's
notations must be followed in interpreting his music.[2]

During the last months of his life Ravel seldom left
the shelter of the little house at Montfort-l'Amaury. He
had planned and decorated it with enthusiasm; now it
became a refuge for his last days and witness to the
silent suffering of its unfortunate master. His efforts to
escape from his affliction through the company of friends
and the bright lights of the city were now over; Ravel
was at last resigned to solitude.

On fair days, when he felt physically able, he found
a certain pleasure in walking through the forest of Rambouillet. He knew every path and tree in these familiar
woods, and just where the wild flowers of the various
seasons bloomed; he loved the birds and never tired of
answering their calls.

On one of his rambles through the forest he discovered
a small, hidden pavilion with pointed roof built a century or more before by the Duc de Penthièvre for Mme
de Lamballe. To Ravel, with his love of detail and all
things minute, the interior, decorated with thousands of
seashells in all shapes and colors, was a place of pure

enchantment. He took Mme Jourdan-Morhange to see it and showed her his discovery with the enthusiasm of a child.[3]

> With what delight he did the honors! . . . One might believe that all the shells of the sea are there, carefully cemented into the walls, doors, floor, and ceiling. . . . Ravel amused himself by trying to recall the name of every shell, and was especially delighted with "*les petits tortillons les plus tortillés!*"

As Ravel's condition grew worse, even the walks through the forest ceased to interest him, and he was no longer able to go into Paris to visit his brother and the Bonnets. He would sit for hours on the balcony of Le Belvédère, staring out at the ancient cathedral and rolling meadows and orchards before him. His face emaciated and lined, his body frail and thin, he remained motionless, silent and absorbed, as if lost in another world. Here Hélène Jourdan-Morhange found him one day.

"*Que faîtes vous là, cher Ravel?*" she asked.

With touching simplicity he replied: "*J'attends. . . .*"

Waiting . . . ! Hoping always that some relief, some cure, would be found for his pathetic disorganization. "*Je m'en vais par morceaux,*" he said. Ravel has been compared, as we have seen, to a Swiss clockmaker. Now the mechanism of his own structure was slowly going to pieces, one bit after another. The clock still functioned —but so slowly, and with such anguished effort. . . . Even his illness seemed to have a "*caractère ravélienne.*"

254

Last photograph of Ravel
(taken two months before
his death) with the pian-
ist Jacques Février

Maurice Ravel on his death-bed.
Sketch by Luc-Albert Moreau

Tomb of Ravel, which he shares with his father and mother in the l[...] cemetery of Levallois-Perret, just outside of Paris

With terrible lucidity he felt the secret springs of his will relax. He knew the torture of being buried alive in an organism no longer obedient to the intelligence. He saw with despair a stranger living within him, to whom he was chained by a malevolent destiny. . . . Seized by an implacable ailment, walled in silence, Maurice Ravel underwent his tragic ordeal with proud and unshaken dignity.[4]

Ravel retained his mental lucidity to the end. If only his reason had gone, it would have been easier for him. Then he would not have been obliged to watch his own dissolution and the ravages of the inexorable disease which slowly invaded his mind and body.

One day he spoke to Hélène Jourdan-Morhange of Chabrier's sad end. "It's terrible, isn't it?" he exclaimed, recalling an incident that happened just before Chabrier's death. "The man witnessed a performance of his *Gwendoline* without recognizing his own music!"

A number of the world's great composers have met with tragic ends. Bach became blind—but he could still dictate his music. Beethoven grew deaf—yet some of his finest works were written after his hearing was gone. Schumann lost his reason, and so did our own Mac-Dowell. Ravel's end, however, was still more unfortunate, for he retained his mental faculties while imprisoned in a completely useless vehicle; his mind remained clear, overflowing with musical ideas, but he could not express them. A bitter sense of frustration—a failure to accomplish what he felt was his destiny—made his last years an unceasing torment. For what greater tragedy

255

than this could exist: to be filled with visions of rare harmonies, to long to share these with the world—and to be denied the power to interpret these visions in material form?

During the fall months of 1937 Ravel grew much weaker. The faithful Mme Reveleau looked after him with devoted care, but there was nothing she could do to rouse him from his mournful abstraction. He never complained, but occasionally he would say, looking out from his balcony: *"Je ne verrai pas ça longtemps!"* or, to his brother, in an unfinished sentence full of meaning: *"Mon pauvre Edouard, quand je ne serai plus là. . . ."*

Edouard eventually called a consultation of the leading Paris brain specialists, and they decided that a cerebral operation was the only remaining hope. A recent case similar to Ravel's (also diagnosed as "shrinking of the brain") had been successfully relieved by injecting a certain fluid into the skull cavity to give nourishment to the receding tissues, and the doctors hoped Ravel might derive benefit from a corresponding operation. But they did not conceal the fact that there were grave dangers attendant on such a delicate adjustment. They consulted Ravel: was he willing to take a chance and undergo an operation which might relieve his intolerable condition, but might—on the other hand—prove fatal?

Edouard was sorely apprehensive; he could not bear to contemplate the possibility of losing his beloved brother. But Maurice did not hesitate. Anything, he felt, was preferable to his present condition. Already he felt himself more dead than alive. . . .

On December 18 they took Ravel to a private hospital on the rue Boileau and prepared him for the operation. He was in better spirits than he had been in for a long time, and laughed when he saw his reflection in the mirror. "I look like a Moor," he exclaimed, pointing to the turban of white bandages that swathed his shaved head.

Dr. Clovis Vincent operated on the morning of December 19. It was not possible, in view of the delicate brain tissue involved, to administer a general anesthetic, and the long hour-and-a-half operation was performed under local anesthesia. Ravel, however, did not suffer; he slipped quietly into a deep sleep and never regained consciousness. In this state he lingered for nearly ten days, and finally in the early morning of December 28 passed quietly away.

XX

FINALE

RAVEL'S FUNERAL——CONCERTS OF HIS
WORKS FOLLOWING HIS DEATH——THE
LAST TRIBUTE OF RICARDO VIÑES——
EULOGIES BY HIS CONTEMPORARIES

EDOUARD RAVEL knew that his brother would not wish an official funeral with all the pomp and ceremony which the French Government usually accords its illustrious dead. Maurice had always tried to avoid publicity and the acclaim of the multitude. His last wish was to be buried quietly next to those who even after they had left him always remained closest to his heart: his father and his mother.

As the year was drawing to its close, on the thirtieth of December, 1937, a modest funeral procession proceeded to the cemetery of Levallois-Perret. In spite of Edouard's efforts to make the occasion as simple as possible, a crowd of friends and devoted admirers gathered to pay their last tribute to the quiet little man whom they had loved, not only for his music, but for himself as well. Many of the younger musicians were there, and also Igor Stravinsky, who was especially affected by the

258

loss of his friend. Jean Zay, Minister of National Education, pronounced, in the name of the French Government, a moving oration over the grave.

By a curious coincidence a broadcast of *L'Enfant et les sortilèges* had been scheduled for December 28, the very evening of Ravel's death. A small group of his most intimate friends and pupils, including Roland-Manuel, Maurice Delage, and Stravinsky, gathered at the *Salle du Conservatoire* to listen to this living voice of their departed master. Manuel Rosenthal directed the Orchestre National with such fervor and emotion that he inspired the singers, chorus, and orchestra with transcendent enthusiasm, and they gave a superlative performance.

This was the first tribute to the departed Ravel, but many others followed: radio festivals, concerts by the great Paris orchestras devoted exclusively to his works, discourses, eulogies, and so on. A few days after Ravel's death Inghelbrecht directed the Orchestre National in another radio concert featuring the Concerto in G with Jean Doyen at the piano, and the *Daphnis and Chloe* suite. The week following, Bigot conducted the Lamoureux Orchestra in a "festival of soloists": Madeleine Grey sang "Shéhérazade"; Jacques Février played the Concerto for left hand, and Lily Laskine the *Introduction and Allegro* for harp; the violinist Schwarz followed with *Tzigane*, and *Bolero* completed the program. On January 19 Marguerite Long played the Concerto in G with the Colonne Orchestra under Paul Paray, in a special festival of Ravel's compositions. All over the world there were concerts devoted to his memory.

One of the most touching tributes came from the little municipality of St-Cloud, where a gala concert, with music and addresses of appreciation, was held at the Mairie next door to the cathedral. Ricardo Viñes, Ravel's oldest friend, contributed to the program, playing an original composition which he had written in memory of Ravel. Some years before, Viñes had composed a *Hommage à Satie,* and he had always wanted to do another piano number in tribute to his friend Maurice. He even began this early in December of 1937, but abandoned it when he found that—for some reason that he could not explain—the work assumed a somber and almost funereal tone. During the days following the sad news of Ravel's death Viñes completed the manuscript and called it *Menuet Spectral—à la mémoire de Maurice Ravel.*

The melancholy grace of the Minuet was in perfect keeping with the spirit of the memorial concert at St-Cloud; the deep tones in the bass of Viñes' composition gave a singular effect of bells tolling. Suddenly the chimes of the cathedral next door began to ring.

They were exactly in tune with the deep tones of the *Menuet Spectral.* "*Même les cloches de l'église pleuraient la mort de l'illustre, de l'immortel Ravel. . . .*"

Many touching tributes have been paid to the memory of Maurice Ravel, including a number of recent biographies—outstanding among these the work of Roland-Manuel—and two volumes of "souvenirs" by friends and intimates of the composer: *Hommage à Maurice Ravel* (special number of the *Revue Musicale*, December 1938) and *Maurice Ravel par quelques-uns de ses familiers*, edited by Roger Wild.

A short biography by Grasset includes the following tribute:[1]

Maurice Ravel was one of the most noble personifications of the French soul. Elegant in his simplicity, disdainful of appearances, . . . faithful in friendships, indulgent to ingratitude, capable of all delicacy and also of all audacity . . . he inspired the beginning of this century with his radiance.

Hélène Jourdan-Morhange says:[2]

His life was a straight line. Just as in his music the minute attention to detail did not lessen the sweep of the general line, so his meticulous daily life did not affect the nobility of his actions.

Jacques de Zogheb, Ravel's neighbor at Montfort-l'Amaury, wrote:[3]

The man had an incomparable greatness of soul. I believe he never told a lie. His integrity, his disdain of honors, touched the sublime.

Léon-Paul Fargue states:[4]

He liked to do, and to do well: everything that came from his brain . . . carries the mark of perfection. . . . His passion was to offer to the public finished works polished to a supreme degree.

FINALE

Roland-Manuel, who through his studies of Ravel perhaps came closer to the composer than any other living person, says:[5]

He had more frankness than elegance; more courtesy than cordiality; more sociability, more humor, than abandon; more devotion to friendship than indulgence in camaraderie, and more ingenuousness than anything else.

He never suspected evil or perfidy. In twenty-six years I have never heard him speak against another. I never knew him to ask for anything for himself except permission to serve his country. . . .

To borrow Ronsard's epitaph, his soul was:

> . . . simple, sans remords
> De meurtre, poison ou rancune,
> Méprisant faveurs et trésors
> Tant enviés par la commune.[6]

ACKNOWLEDGMENTS

IN December 1938 and January 1939, a number of French biographies of Maurice Ravel appeared in Paris. Until that time, however, no printed information had existed concerning the great French composer except a number of articles in various periodicals and newspapers, and two monographs by Roland-Manuel (*Maurice Ravel et son œuvre*, 1914 and 1926, and *M. Ravel et son œuvre dramatique*).

When this present American biography was begun early in 1938, shortly after Ravel's death, it was thus necessary to obtain most of the information at first hand, from those who had been close to the celebrated musician. His intimate friends were few in number, and of his immediate family there is only one member surviving, his brother Edouard. Special thanks are due to Elizabeth C. Moore who rendered invaluable service in research work and in helping to edit and prepare this manuscript.

The author gratefully acknowledges the invaluable and kindly assistance of Edouard Ravel, who opened "Le Belvédère" for the first time after his brother's death and allowed pictures to be taken there, also donating many rare and unpublished photographs. M. and Mme Bonnet and Jacques de Zogheb had much to say about the long years during which they had known Ravel, while Mme Reveleau, the faithful *bonne*, told of the fifteen years she had served the composer. With characteristic amiability Ricardo Viñes unlocked vast storehouses of early memories about his lifelong friend Maurice. Maurice Delage, G. Jean-Aubry, and Henri Février, all well known in the musical and literary circles of Paris, gave valuable information, while the latter's talented son, the pianist Jacques Février, was especially helpful in making it

ACKNOWLEDGMENTS

possible to reach several of Ravel's intimates. Two outstanding French cellists, Maurice Maréchal and Gérard Hekking, supplied amusing details of their tours with Ravel.

Mme Jourdan-Morhange, music critic of note, was most generous in lending unusual photographs and in furnishing revealing details of Ravel's personality and character. Mme Marguerite Long, the concert pianist and head of the Paris Conservatory's piano department, related incidents of her association with the master, and donated one of the last pictures taken of Ravel, showing the two friends together at St-Jean-de-Luz.

In the United States Mr. and Mrs. E. Robert Schmitz graciously opened their files and produced valuable details about the American tour. Hans Kindler, distinguished conductor of the National Orchestra at Washington, D. C., told interesting anecdotes of his friendship with Ravel, as did Adolf Bolm, the well-known dancer, and the American composer Alexander Steinert.

Without the friendly help of all of these, the present volume would not have been possible; the author hopes that each will feel a share in the creation of this the first biography written in English about Maurice Ravel.

LIST OF RAVEL'S COMPOSITIONS

1893   *Sérénade grotesque.* (Piano.)
        Unpublished.
1894   "Ballade de la reine morte d'aimer." (Voice and
            piano.)
        Words by Roland de Marès.
        Unpublished.
1895   "Un grand sommeil noir." (Voice and piano.)
        Words by Verlaine.
        Unpublished.
        Menuet antique. (Piano.) (Orchestrated.)
        Dedicated to Ricardo Viñes.
        Published by Enoch.
        First performance April 13, 1901, by Viñes. So-
            ciété Nationale.
1896   *Sites Auriculaires.* (Two pianos, 4 hands.)
            1. Habanera (1895).
            2. Entre Cloches (1896).
        Unpublished.
        First performance March 5, 1898, by Viñes and
            Mlle Dron. Société Nationale.
        "Sainte." (Voice and piano.)
        Words by Mallarmé.
        Dedicated to Mme E. Bonniot (née Mallarmé).
        Published by Durand.
1898   "Deux Epigrammes." (Voice and piano.)
        Words by Marot.
        Dedicated to M. Hardy Thé.
        Published by Demets.
        First performance January 27, 1900, by Hardy
            Thé. Société Nationale.

Shéhérazade. (Overture for Orchestra.)
  Unpublished.
  First performance May 27, 1899, Ravel conducting. Société Nationale.

1899   *Pavane pour une Infante défunte.*
  Published by Demets.
  First performance April 5, 1902, by Viñes. Société Nationale.

"Si morne." (Voice and piano.)
  Words by Verhaeren.
  Unpublished.

1901   *Myrrha.* (Cantata for Prix de Rome contest, 1901.)
  Words by Beissier.
  Unpublished.

Jeux d'eau. (Piano.)
  Dedicated to "mon cher maître Gabriel Fauré."
  Published by Demets.
  First performance April 5, 1902, by Viñes. Société Nationale.

1902   *Alcyone.* (Cantata for Prix de Rome contest, 1902.)
  Words by A. and F. Adenis.
  Unpublished.

1902–3   *Quatuor à cordes.* (String quartet.)
  Dedicated to "mon cher maître Gabriel Fauré."
  Published by Durand.
  First performance March 5, 1904, by Heyman Quartet. Société Nationale.

1903   *Alyssa.* (Cantata for Prix de Rome contest, 1903.)
  Unpublished.

"Manteau de fleurs." (Voice and piano.) (Orchestrated.)
  Words by Paul Gravollet.
  Published by Hamelle.

"Shéhérazade." (Voice and orchestra.)
  Words by Tristan Klingsor.
    1. Asie. (Dedicated to Mme J. Hatto.)

266

2. La Flûte enchantée. (Dedicated to Mme de St-Marceaux.)

3. L'Indifférent. (Dedicated to Mme S. Bardac.)

Published by Durand.

First performance May 17, 1904, by Mme J. Hatto, Cortot conducting. Société Nationale.

1905 "Le Noël des jouets." (Voice and piano.) (Orchestrated.)

Words by Maurice Ravel.

Dedicated to Mme J. Cruppi.

Published by Mathot.

Sonatine. (Piano.) (Orchestrated.)

Dedicated to Ida and Cipa Godebski.

Published by Durand.

First performance March 10, 1906, by Mme de Lestang. Lyons.

Miroirs. (Suite for piano.)

1. Noctuelles. (Dedicated to Léon-Paul Fargue.)

2. Oiseaux tristes. (Dedicated to Ricardo Viñes.)

3. Une barque sur l'océan. (Dedicated to Paul Sordes.) (Orchestrated.)

4. Alborada del Gracioso. (Dedicated to M. D. Calvocoressi.) (Orchestrated.)

5. La Vallée des cloches. (Dedicated to Maurice Delage.)

Published by Demets.

First performance January 6, 1906, by Viñes. Société Nationale.

1905–6 *Introduction et Allegro* for harp with accompaniment of string quartet, flute, and clarinet.

Dedicated to M. Albert Bondel.

Published by Durand.

First performance February 22, 1907, by Mlle Micheline Kahn. Cercle Musical.

LIST OF RAVEL'S COMPOSITIONS

1906   "Les Grands Vents venus d'Outre-Mer." (Voice and
           piano.)
        Words by Henri de Régnier.
        Dedicated to Jacques Durand.
        Published by Durand.
        "Histoires naturelles." (Voice and piano.) (Orches-
           trated by Manuel Rosenthal.)
        Words by Jules Renard.
            1. Le Paon. (Dedicated to Mme J. Bathori.)
            2. Le Grillon. (Dedicated to Mlle Madeleine
               Picard.)
            3. Le Cygne. (Dedicated to Mme Edwards née
               Godebska.)
            4. Le Martin-Pêcheur. (Dedicated to M. Emile
               Engel.)
            5. La Pintade. (Dedicated to M. Roger-Ducasse.)
        Published by Durand.
        First performance January 13, 1907, by Mme
           Bathori. Société Nationale.
1907   "Sur l'Herbe." (Voice and piano.)
        Words by Verlaine.
        Published by Durand.
        "Vocalise en forme d'Habanera." (Voice.)
        Published by Leduc.
        "Cinq mélodies populaires grecques." * (Voice and
           piano.)
        Words by Calvocoressi.
            1. Le réveil de la mariée.
            2. Là-bas vers l'église.
            3. Quel galant!
            4. Chanson des cueilleuses de lentisque.
            5. Tout gai!
        Published by Durand.

   * Numbers 1 and 5 orchestrated by Ravel; 2, 3, and 4 by Rosenthal. A sixth, "Tripatos," added later, has never been published.
268

Rapsodie espagnole. (Orchestra.)
1. Prélude à la nuit.
2. Malagueña.
3. Habanera.
4. Feria.

Dedicated to "mon cher maître Charles de Bériot."
Published by Durand.
First performance March 19, 1908, E. Colonne
conducting. Concerts Colonne.

L'Heure espagnole. (Comedy-opera in one act.)
Words by Franc-Nohain.
Dedicated to Mme J. Cruppi.
Published by Durand.
First performance May 19, 1911. Opéra-Comique,
Paris.

1908 *Ma Mère l'Oye.* (For children, piano 4 hands.) (Orchestrated.)
1. Pavane de la Belle au bois dormant.
2. Petit Poucet.
3. Laideronnette, Impératrice des Pagodes.
4. La Belle et la Bête.
5. Le Jardin féerique.

Dedicated to Mimie and Jean Godebski.
Published by Durand.
First performance April 20, 1910. Société Musi-
cale Indépendante.

Gaspard de la Nuit. (Suite for piano.)
From poems by Aloysius Bertrand.
1. Ondine. (Dedicated to Harold Bauer.)
2. Le Gibet. (Dedicated to Jean Marnold.)
3. Scarbo. (Dedicated to Rudolph Ganz.)

Published by Durand.
First performance January 9, 1909, by Viñes. Société Nationale.

1909 *Menuet sur le nom d'Haydn.* (Piano.)
Published by Durand.

1910   "Chants populaires." (Voice and piano.)
1. Chanson française.
2. Chanson espagnole.
3. Chanson italienne.
4. Chanson hébraïque. (Orchestrated.)
5. Chanson écossaise. (Unpublished.)
6. Chanson flamande. (Unpublished.)
7. Chanson russe. (Unpublished.)
Published by Jurgenson 1910, Durand 1925.

1911   *Valses nobles et sentimentales.* (Piano.) (Orchestrated.)
Dedicated to Louis Aubert.
Published by Durand.
First performance 1911, by Louis Aubert. Société Musicale Indépendante.

1909–12 *Daphnis et Chloé.* ("Symphonie chorégraphique," ballet and orchestra.)
Based on Michel Fokine's adaptation of a Longus fable.
Dedicated to Serge Diaghileff.
Published by Durand.
First performance June 18, 1912, with Nijinsky, Karsavina, and Bolm, Pierre Monteux conducting. Grande Saison de Paris.

1912   *Ma Mère l'Oye.* (In ballet form—orchestrated.)
Dedicated to Jacques Rouché.
Published by Durand.
First performance January, 1912. Théâtre des Arts.
Adélaïde, ou le langage des fleurs. (Ballet from *Valses nobles et sentimentales.*)
Published by Durand.
First performance April 22, 1912, by Mlle Trouhanova, Ravel conducting.

270

1913   "Trois poèmes de Stéphane Mallarmé." (Voice with piano, two flutes, and two clarinets.)

Words by Mallarmé.

    1. Soupir. (Dedicated to Igor Stravinsky.)
    2. Placet futile. (Dedicated to Florent Schmitt.)
    3. Surgi de la croupe et du bond. (Dedicated to Erik Satie.)

Published by Durand.

First performance January 14, 1914, by Mme Bathori. Société Musicale Indépendante.

A la manière de . . . (Piano.)

    1. Borodine.
    2. Chabrier.

Published by Mathot.

Prélude. (Piano.)

Dedicated to Mlle J. Leleu.

Published by Durand.

1914   "Deux mélodies hébraïques." (Voice and piano.) (Orchestrated.)

    1. Kaddisch.
    2. L'Enigme éternelle.

Dedicated to Mme Alvina-Alvi.

Published by Durand.

Trio. (Piano, violin, and cello.)

Dedicated to Henri Gédalge.

Published by Durand.

1915   "Trois Chansons." (Mixed chorus without accompaniment.)

Words by Maurice Ravel.

    1. Nicolette. (Dedicated to Tristan Klingsor.)
    2. Trois beaux oiseaux du Paradis. (Dedicated to Paul Painlevé.)
    3. Ronde. (Dedicated to Mme Paul Clemenceau.)

Published by Durand.

LIST OF RAVEL'S COMPOSITIONS

1917   *Le Tombeau de Couperin.* (Suite for piano.) (Orchestrated.)

       1. Prélude. (A la mémoire du lieutenant Jacques Charlot.)

      * 2. Fugue. (A la mémoire du sous-lieutenant Jean Cruppi.)

       3. Forlane. (A la mémoire du lieutenant Gabriel Deluc.)

       4. Rigaudon. (A la mémoire de Jean Dreyfus.)

       5. Menuet. (A la mémoire de Pierre et Pascal Gaudin.)

      * 6. Toccata. (A la mémoire de Jean de Marliave.)

      Published by Durand.

      First performance April, 1919. Salle Gaveau, Paris.

1918   *Frontispice.* (Piano, 4 hands.)

      Published by *Les Feuillets d'Art.*

1919–20 *La Valse.* (*"Poème chorégraphique"* for orchestra.)

      Dedicated to Misia Sert.

      Published by Durand.

      First performance January 8, 1920. Concerts Lamoureux.

1920–22 *Sonate en quatre parties.* (Violin and cello.)

      Dedicated "A la mémoire de Claude Debussy."

      Published by Durand.

1922   *Berceuse sur le nom de Gabriel Fauré.* (Violin and piano.)

      Dedicated to Claude Roland-Manuel.

      Published by Durand.

1924   "Ronsard à son âme." (Voice and piano.)

      Words by Ronsard.

      Dedicated to Marcelle Gérard.

      Published by Durand.

* Not orchestrated.

Tzigane—Rapsodie de concert. (Violin and piano.)
   Dedicated to Jelly d'Aranyi.
   Published by Durand.

1925 *L'Enfant et les sortilèges.* (One-act fantasy.)
   Words by Colette.
   Published by Durand.
   First performance March 21, 1925. Théâtre de
      Monte-Carlo.

1925–6 "Chansons madécasses." (Voice with piano, flute, and
      cello.)
   Words by Evariste Parny.
      1. Nadanhove.
      2. Aoua!
      3. Il est doux . . .
   Dedicated to Mrs. Elizabeth Sprague Coolidge.
   Published by Durand.
   First performance October, 1925, with Mme
      Bathori; Ravel, piano; Hans Kindler, cello;
      Fleury, flute. Hotel Majestic, Paris.

1927 "Rêves." (Voice and piano.)
   Words by Léon-Paul Fargue.
   Published by Durand.
   Sonate en trois parties. (Violin and piano.)
   Dedicated to Hélène Jourdan-Morhange.
   Published by Durand.
   L'Eventail de Jeanne—Fanfare. (Orchestra.)
   Published by Heugel.

1928 *Bolero.* (Orchestra.)
   Published by Durand.
   First performance November 20, 1928, by Mme
      Ida Rubinstein.

1931 *Concerto en trois parties.* (Piano and orchestra.)
   Dedicated to Mme Marguerite Long.
   Published by Durand.
   First performance November 11, 1931, by Mme
      Long, Ravel conducting. Salle Pleyel, Paris.

Concerto pour main gauche. (Piano—left hand—and orchestra.)

Dedicated to Paul Wittgenstein.

Published by Durand.

First performance November 27, 1931, by Wittgenstein. Vienna.

1932   "Don Quichotte à Dulcinée." (Voice and piano.)

Words by P. Morand.

1. Chanson romantique.
2. Chanson épique.
3. Chanson à boire.

Published by Durand.

RECORDINGS OF RAVEL'S WORKS

Note.—Following are the best recordings available in the United States at the time this book went to press, December 1939. A few other recordings exist, made by European companies; for information about these consult your record dealer.

Abbreviations

B Brunswick	G His Master's Voice (Victor
C Columbia	in Europe)
CM Columbia Masterwork set	O Odeon
D Decca	V Victor
	VM Victor Musical Master-
	piece album

Alborada del Gracioso—*see* Songs
Berceuse sur le nom de Gabriel Fauré.
Marcel Darrieux, violin, with
piano acc. (*With* Dussek: Minuet)　　O 166322　$1.50
Bolero
For orchestra:
—Lamoureux Orchestra, cond. by
Ravel. Two records, four sides...　B 90039/40　3.00
—Amsterdam Concertgebouw, cond.
by Mengelberg. Two records, four
sides ....　C 67890/1　3.00
—Boston Symphony, cond. by Kous-
sevitzky. Two records, three sides
(*with* Satie-Debussy; Gymnopédie)　V 7251/2　4.00
—Boston "Pops," cond. by Fiedler.
Two records, three sides (*with* Hal-
vorsen: Entry of the Boyards) ...　VM 552　3.50

RECORDINGS OF RAVEL'S WORKS

For piano:

—Morton Gould. (*With* Gould: Satirical Dance) ....   V 24205 $ .75

—Fray and Braggiotti, two pianos..   V 24563   .75

Chansons madécasses, etc.—*see* Songs

Concerto for Piano and Orchestra. Marguerite Long and symphony orchestra, cond. by Ravel. Three records, five sides (*with* Ravel: Pavane pour une Infante défunte) ...   CM 176   4.50

Concerto for Piano, left hand alone. Jacqueline Blancquard and Paris Philharmonic Orchestra, cond. by Münch. Two records, four sides..   D-X 204/5   4.00

Daphnis and Chloe. Ballet

Suite No. 1 (Nocturne *and* Danse guerrière only). Paris Conservatory Orchestra, cond. by Coppola.....   V 11882   1.50

Suite No. 2. Boston Symphony, cond. by Koussevitzky. Two records, four sides ....   V 7143/4   4.00

—Straram Orchestra, cond. by Gaubert. Two records, four sides....   C 67827/8   3.00

Don Quichotte à Dulcinée—*see* Songs

L'Enfant et les sortilèges. One-act fantasy

Foxtrot "Five O'Clock" arr. by Branga (labeled on the American pressing "Dream of a Naughty Boy"). Symphony orchestra, cond. by Coppola. (*With* Ravel: Pavane pour une Infante défunte) ....   V 9306   1.50

Gaspard de la Nuit. Piano. (Both recordings complete)

—Jean Doyen. Three records, six sides.. G-DA 4906/7

                                           G-DB 5043   6.50

RECORDINGS OF RAVEL'S WORKS

—Walter Gieseking. Two records, four
sides .... CM-X 141 $3.50
Habanera—*see* Pièce en forme de Habanera, *and* Rapsodie espagnole,
whose third part is a Habanera
L'Heure espagnole. Opera in one act. So-
loists and symphony orchestra,
cond. by Truc. Seven records, fourteen sides .... C album 14.00
—Soprano aria, Scene 12, "Oh! la pi-
toyable aventure." Fanny Heldy.
(*With* "Restons ici" from Manon) G-DB 1512 2.50
Histoires naturelles—*see* Songs
Introduction and Allegro. String quartet,
harp, flute, clarinet
—Virtuoso Quartet, with Cockerill,
Murchie, Draper. Two records,
three sides (*with* Bridge: Novelette
No. 3) .... V 9738/9 3.00
—Denise Herbrecht (harp) and en-
semble dir. by Coppola. Two rec-
ords, three sides (*with* Debussy:
Arabesque) .... G-L 903/4 4.00
Jeux d'eau. Piano
—Alfred Cortot (*with* Ravel: Sonatine,
Pt. 3) .... V 7729 2.00
—Robert Casadesus................ C 2080M .75
—B. Moiseivitch (*with* Brahms: E-flat
Rhapsody) .... G D1648 2.50
—Marie Thérèse Brazeau (*with* De-
bussy: Feu d'artifice) .... B 90113 1.50
Ma Mère l'Oye. Suite for orchestra
—Paris Conservatory Orchestra, cond.
by Coppola. Two records, four
sides ....G-DB 4898/9 5.00

277

RECORDINGS OF RAVEL'S WORKS

—Lamoureux Orchestra, cond. by
    Wolff. Two records, four sides... B 90342/3 $3.00
—Boston Symphony, cond. by Kous-
    sevitzky. Two records, four sides.. V 7370/1 4.00
—Columbia Broadcasting Symphony
    Orchestra, cond. by Howard Bar-
    low. Two records, four sides..... CM-X 151 3.50

Menuet antique, arr. for orchestra

—Lamoureux Orchestra, cond. by Wolff B 90099 1.50
—Symphony orchestra, cond. by Cop-
    pola .... V 11133 1.50

Miroirs. Piano suite of five pieces, of
    which only three have been re-
    corded; and of these only one is
    now available:

Alborada del Gracioso. Jesus Maria
    Sanromá, piano................ V 4425 1.00
—Orchestral arr. Minneapolis Sym-
    phony Orchestra, cond. by Or-
    mandy .... V 8552 2.00
—Same. Straram Orchestra, cond. by
    Straram .... C 68077D 1.50

Pavane pour une Infante défunte. Piano
Myra Hess...................... C 4082M 1.00
Marguerite Long (*with* Ravel: Con-
    certo for Piano, CM 176, q.v.)
Orchestral arr. Colonne Orchestra, cond.
    by Pierne..................... C-G 67785D 1.50
—Berlin Philharmonic, cond. by
    Wolff (*with* Fauré: Sicilienne from
    Pelléas et Mélisande) .... B 90149 1.50

Pièce en forme de Habanera. Vocalise
    (wordless song)
Piano arr. Mieczyslaw Münz. (*With*
    Scriabin: Etude in C-sharp minor) D 20301   .50

Violin and piano. Mischa Elman, violin, with piano acc. (*With* Saint-Saëns: Le Cygne) . . . .   V 1592 $1.50

Cello and piano. Horace Britt, cello, with piano acc. (*With* Nín: Granadina) . . . .   C 192M   .75

Rapsodie espagnole. Orchestra

—Lamoureux Orchestra, cond. by Wolff. Two records, four sides. . . .   B 90340/1   3.00

—Philadelphia Orchestra, cond. by Stokowski. Two records, four sides   V 8282/3   4.00

Ronsard à son âme—*see* Songs

Shéhérazade—*see* Songs

Sonatine. Piano

—Alfred Cortot. Two records, three sides (*with* Ravel: Jeux d'eau) . . .   V 7728/9   4.00

—Franz Josef Hirt. Two records, three sides (*with* Debussy: La Puerta dal Vino) . . . .   G-B 4127/8   3.00

Songs

Don Quichotte à Dulcinée. Three songs. Martial Singher (baritone) with orchestra cond. by Coppola. Two records, three sides (*with* Ravel: Ronsard à son âme) . . . .   V 4404/5   2.00

Histoires naturelles

Complete (five songs). Suzanne Stappen (soprano) and Marius-François Gaillard (piano). Three records, six sides. . . . .   O 188903/5   6.00

Le Paon, Le Grillon, Le Martin-Pêcheur. Jane Bathori (soprano) with piano acc. . . . .   C 15179   2.00

Ronsard à son âme—*see* Don Quichotte, above

Shéhérazade. One song recorded:

RECORDINGS OF RAVEL'S WORKS

La flûte enchantée. Rose Walter (soprano) with orchestra. In Columbia History of Music album only ..   C DB1301
                                    (consult dealer)

Trois chansons. Les Chanteurs de Lyon (unacc. chorus) . . . .   C 9136M $1.50

Trois chansons hébraïques. Madeleine Grey (soprano), Ravel (piano) ..   B 85022   1.25

Trois chansons madécasses. Madeleine Grey (soprano), acc. by Ravel (piano), violin, and cello. Two records, four sides . . . .   B 85032/3   2.50

String Quartet

—Pro Arte Quartet. Four records, eight sides . . . .   VM 400   8.00

—Lener Quartet. Four records, eight sides . . . .   CM 208   6.00

—Krettly Quartet. Three records, six sides . . . .   VM 88   5.00

Le Tombeau de Couperin. Suite for piano. Madeleine de Valmalete. Three records, six sides . . . .   B 85027/8
                                    B 90337   4.00

Orchestral arr. Paris Conservatory Orchestra, cond. by Coppola. Two records, four sides . . . .   V 12320/1 *   3.00

Trio. Henry Merckel (violin), Marcelli-Herson (cello), Eliane Zurfluh-Tenroc (piano). Three records, six sides . . . .   VM 129   5.00

Tzigane (Rapsodie de concert). Violin and piano

—Zino Francescatti and M. Fauré . . . .   C 68102D   1.50

* This recording, made in 1938, is apparently nothing more than a reissue of the 1931 recording, by the same orchestra and the same conductor, V 11150/1, $3.00.

—Jascha Heifetz and Arpad Sandor...	V 8411	$2.00
—Yehudi Menuhin and A. Balsam....	V 7810	2.00

La Valse (Poème chorégraphique). Orchestra

—Lamoureux Orchestra, cond. by Wolff. Two records, four sides.... B 90186/7 3.00

—Boston Symphony, cond. by Koussevitzky. Two records, three sides (*with* Debussy-Ravel: Danse) .... V 7413/4 4.00

—Paris Conservatory Orchestra, cond. by Gaubert. Two records, four sides .... C 67384/5D 3.00

Valses nobles et sentimentales. Orchestra. Paris Conservatory Orchestra, cond. by Coppola. Two records, four sides .... V 11727/8 3.00

Vocalise—*see* Pièce en forme de Habanera

BIBLIOGRAPHY

Books Used in Preparing This Work

Claude Roland-Manuel—*Maurice Ravel et son œuvre*, 1914 (revised 1926), Durand et Cie, 4 Place de la Madeleine, Paris

—— *M. Ravel et son œuvre dramatique*, 1928, Editions Musicales de la Librairie de France, 110 Boulevard St-Germain, Paris

—— *A la gloire de Ravel*, 1938, Editions de la Nouvelle Revue Critique, 12 rue Chanoinesse, Paris

Roger Wild, editor—*Maurice Ravel par quelquesuns de ses familiers*, 1939, Editions du Tambourinaire, 186 rue du Faubourg St-Honoré, Paris

Grasset—*Maurice Ravel*, 1938, Editions Bernard Grasset, 61 rue des Saints-Pères, Paris

P. D. Templier—*Erik Satie*, 1932, Les Editions Rieder, 7 Place Saint-Sulpice, Paris

P. Fauré-Fremiet—*Gabriel Fauré*, 1929, Les Editions Rieder, 7 Place Saint-Sulpice, Paris

Oscar Thompson—*Debussy, Man and Artist*, 1937, Dodd, Mead & Co., New York

Léon Vallas—*Claude Debussy, His Life and His Works*, 1933, Oxford University Press, London

Marion Bauer—*Twentieth Century Music*, 1934, G. P. Putnam's Sons, New York

Daniel Gregory Mason—*Music in My Time, and Other Reminiscences*, 1938, Macmillan, New York

G. Jean-Aubry—*French Music of To-day*, translated by Edwin Evans, 1919, Kegan Paul, London

Colette—*L'Enfant et les sortilèges*, fantaisie lyrique en deux parties, 1925, Durand et Cie, Paris

BIBLIOGRAPHY

Periodicals Used in Preparing This Work

Revue Musicale, Special number dedicated to Maurice Ravel, April 1925, Editions de la Nouvelle Revue Française, 3 rue de Grenelle, Paris

Revue Musicale, Special number: "Hommage à Maurice Ravel," December 1938, La Revue Musicale, 70 Avenue Kléber, Paris (containing the autobiographical sketch dictated by Ravel to Roland-Manuel in 1928)

L'Echo des Concours, February 1938

The Chesterian (English musical magazine), January-February 1938

Nouvelle revue française, February 1910; July 1911

Les Cahiers d'aujourd'hui, 1922, No. 10

London *Daily Telegraph,* two interviews, dates unknown

Le Temps, June 13, 1899; May 28, 1911

La Liberté, February 5, 1907

Mercure de France, April 16, 1908; August 16, 1917

Boston *Evening Transcript,* January 13, 1928

New York *Times,* January 16, 1928

284

SOURCE NOTES

CHAPTER I

NOTE
1. Ravel, in a London *Daily Telegraph* interview, quoted by David Bruno Ussher in the Los Angeles *Evening Express*, August 8, 1928
2. Ravel, quoted by Joaquin Nín in "Comment est né le Bolero de Ravel," *Revue Musicale*, December 1938
3. Ravel, in an autobiographical sketch dictated to Roland-Manuel in 1928 (printed in the *Revue Musicale*, December 1938)
4. André Suarèz, "Esquisse" in *Revue Musicale*, December 1938

CHAPTER II

1. Ravel, autobiographical sketch, 1928
2. Charles-René, quoted by Roland-Manuel in *Maurice Ravel et son œuvre* (by permission of the publishers, Durand et Cie)

CHAPTER III

1. G. Jean-Aubry, *French Music of To-day* (by permission of E. P. Dutton & Co.)
2. Ricardo Viñes, "Fragments," in *Revue Musicale*, December 1938
3. Gustave Mouchet, in *L'Echo des Concours*, February 1938

CHAPTER IV

1. P. D. Templier, *Erik Satie* (by permission of the publishers, Editions Rieder)

285

SOURCE NOTES

NOTE

2. *Ibid.*
3. *Ibid.*
4. Roland-Manuel, *A la gloire de Ravel* (by permission of the publishers, Editions de la Nouvelle Revue Critique)
5. *Ibid.*

CHAPTER V

1. Ph. Fauré-Fremiet, *Gabriel Fauré* (by permission of the publishers, Editions Rieder)
2. *Ibid.*
3. *Ibid.*
4. Roland-Manuel, *A la gloire de Ravel*
5. Pierre Lalo, in *Le Temps*, June 13, 1899
6. Roland-Manuel, *A la gloire de Ravel*
7. Charles Oulmont, "Souvenirs," in *Revue Musicale*, December 1938.

CHAPTER VI

1. Ravel, quoted by Roland-Manuel in *A la gloire de Ravel*
2. Ravel, *ibid.*
3. Romain Rolland, quoted by Marguerite Long in "Souvenirs de Maurice Ravel," *Revue Musicale*, December 1938
4. Ravel, autobiographical sketch, 1928
5. Roland-Manuel, *Maurice Ravel et son œuvre*

CHAPTER VII

1. Maurice Delage, "Les premiers amis de Ravel," in *Maurice Ravel par quelquesuns de ses familiers* (by permission of the publishers, Editions du Tambourinaire)
2. Roland-Manuel, *A la gloire de Ravel*
3. Gaston Carraud, in *La Liberté*, February 5, 1907

NOTE
4. Pierre Lalo, quoted by Roland-Manuel in *Maurice Ravel et son œuvre*

CHAPTER VIII

1. Debussy, quoted by Léon Vallas in *Claude Debussy, His Life and His Works* (by permission of the publishers, Oxford University Press)
2. Oscar Thompson, *Debussy, Man and Artist* (by permission of the publishers, Dodd, Mead & Co.)
3. *Ibid.*
4. Marion Bauer, *Twentieth Century Music* (by permission of the publishers, G. P. Putnam's Sons)
5. Debussy, quoted by Léon Vallas, *op. cit.*
6. Arthur Hoérée, "La Mélodie et l'œuvre lyrique," in *Revue Musicale*, April 1925

CHAPTER IX

1. Maurice Delage, "Les premiers amis de Ravel," in *Maurice Ravel par quelquesuns de ses familiers*
2. Ravel, quoted by Maurice Delage, *ibid.*
3. Jules Renard, quoted by Roland-Manuel in *A la gloire de Ravel*
4. Henri Ghéon, in *Nouvelle revue française*, July 1, 1911
5. Jean Marnold, in *Mercure de France*, August 16, 1917
6. Emile Vuillermoz, "L'Œuvre de Maurice Ravel," in *Maurice Ravel par quelquesuns de ses familiers*
7. Emile Vuillermoz, "Le style orchestral," in *Revue Musicale*, April 1925

CHAPTER X

1. André Suarèz, "Pour Ravel," in *Revue Musicale*, April 1925
2. Jean Marnold, in *Mercure de France*, April 16, 1908

SOURCE NOTES

NOTE

3. Jacques Rivière, in *Nouvelle revue française*, February 1910

4. Ferdinand Hérold, "Souvenirs," in *Revue Musicale*, December 1938

5. Ravel, quoted by Maurice Delage in *Maurice Ravel par quelquesuns de ses familiers*

6. *Ibid.*

7. Roland-Manuel, *A la gloire de Ravel*

8. Emile Vuillermoz, in *Revue Musicale*, April 1925

9. The speeches quoted from *L'Heure espagnole* are translated by the author from the French libretto published by Durand et Cie

10. Pierre Lalo, in *Le Temps*, May 28, 1911

11. *Ibid.*

12. Emile Vuillermoz, in *Revue Musicale*, April 1925

CHAPTER XI

1. Mimie Godebska Blacque-Belair, "Quelques souvenirs intimes sur Ravel," in *Revue Musicale*, December 1938

2. Daniel Gregory Mason, *Music in My Time* (by permission of the publishers, The Macmillan Co.)

3. Roland-Manuel, *A la gloire de Ravel*

4. Alfred Cortot, quoted by Roland-Manuel, *ibid.*

5. Henri Gil-Marchex, "La technique de piano," in *Revue Musicale*, April 1925

6. Emile Vuillermoz, in *Les Cahiers d'aujourd'hui*, 1922, No. 10

CHAPTER XII

1. Colette, "Un salon de musique en 1900," in *Maurice Ravel par quelquesuns de ses familiers*

2. *Ibid.*

3. Ravel, autobiographical sketch, 1928

4. Jean Marnold, in *Mercure de France*, August 16, 1917

CHAPTER XIII

NOTE

1. Ravel, autobiographical sketch, 1928
2. Roland-Manuel, *A la gloire de Ravel*
3. Tristan Klingsor, "L'Epoque Ravel," in *Maurice Ravel par quelquesuns de ses familiers*

CHAPTER XIV

1. Madeleine Grey, "Souvenirs," in *Revue Musicale,* December 1938
2. Ravel, quoted by Roland-Manuel in *A la gloire de Ravel*
3. *Ibid.*
4. *Ibid.*
5. *Ibid.*
6. Hélène Jourdan-Morhange, "Ravel à Montfort-l'Amaury," in *Maurice Ravel par quelquesuns de ses familiers*
7. Ravel, quoted by Georgette Marnold, "Quelques lettres de Maurice Ravel," in *Revue Musicale,* December 1938
8. *Ibid.*
9. Ravel, quoted by Roland-Manuel in *A la gloire de Ravel*
10. Ravel, quoted, *ibid.*
11. Ravel, quoted, *ibid.*
12. Ravel, quoted, *ibid.*
13. Roland-Manuel, *M. Ravel et son œuvre dramatique* (by permission of the publishers, Editions Musicales de la Librairie de France)
14. *Ibid.*

CHAPTER XV

1. Ravel, quoted by Roland-Manuel in *A la gloire de Ravel*
2. Paul Stéfan, "Quelques souvenirs sur Ravel," in *Revue Musicale,* December 1938
3. Madeleine Grey, "Souvenirs," *ibid.*
4. *Ibid.*
5. Ravel, quoted by Roland-Manuel in *A la gloire de Ravel*

SOURCE NOTES

NOTE

6. G. Jean-Aubry, in *The Chesterian,* January-February 1938
7. Roland-Manuel, *A la gloire de Ravel*
8. *Ibid.*
9. Arthur Honegger, quoted by Roland-Manuel, *ibid.*
10. Roland-Manuel, *ibid.*
11. Ravel, quoted by Roland-Manuel, *ibid.*
12. The passages quoted are from Colette's libretto for *L'Enfant et les sortilèges,* by permission of the publishers, Durand et Cie

CHAPTER XVI

1. Roland-Manuel, *A la gloire de Ravel*

CHAPTER XVII

1. H. T. Parker, in the Boston *Evening Transcript,* January 13, 1928
2. Olin Downes, in the New York *Times,* January 16, 1928

CHAPTER XVIII

1. Ravel, in the London *Daily Telegraph,* quoted by Roland-Manuel in *A la gloire de Ravel*

CHAPTER XIX

1. Grasset, *Maurice Ravel*
2. Madeleine Grey, "Souvenirs d'une interprète," in *Revue Musicale,* December 1938
3. Hélène Jourdan-Morhange, "Mon ami Ravel," *ibid.*
4. Emile Vuillermoz, "Maurice Ravel," *ibid.*

Chapter XX

NOTE
1. Grasset, *Maurice Ravel*
2. Hélène Jourdan-Morhange, "Ravel à Montfort-l'Amaury," in *Maurice Ravel par quelquesuns de ses familiers*
3. Jacques de Zogheb, "Souvenirs ravéliens," *ibid.*
4. Léon-Paul Fargue, "Autour de Ravel," *ibid.*
5. Roland-Manuel, *A la gloire de Ravel*
6. Roland-Manuel, "Des valses à *La Valse*," in *Maurice Ravel par quelquesuns de ses familiers*

GENERAL INDEX

293

GENERAL INDEX

GENERAL INDEX

INDEX OF RAVEL'S COMPOSITIONS

INDEX OF RAVEL'S COMPOSITIONS

INDEX OF RAVEL'S COMPOSITIONS

CPSIA information can be obtained
at www.ICGtesting.com
Printed in the USA
LVHW04s2302140518
577225LV00001B/84/P